ARIEL KARMELI

The Courage to Be Simple

144 Reflections on Loving the Truth of Who You Are

First published by Ariel Karmeli 2026

Copyright © 2026 by Ariel Karmeli

All rights reserved. No part of this publication may be reproduced, stored or transmitted in any form or by any means, electronic, mechanical, photocopying, recording, scanning, or otherwise without written permission from the publisher. It is illegal to copy this book, post it to a website, or distribute it by any other means without permission.

Ariel Karmeli asserts the moral right to be identified as the author of this work.

First edition

ISBN: 979-8-9940612-0-6

This book was professionally typeset on Reedsy.
Find out more at reedsy.com

Contents

Dedication	1
Preface	2
Acknowledgments	5
Introduction - Embracing Life's Dualities: An Invitation	7
Part I - Reflections on Personality and Life's Dualities	11
Introduction	11
Chapter 1: Finding the Self Beneath the Self	14
Understanding Begins with Accepting Limits	14
The Limits That Make Freedom Real	15
Perspectives Keep on Shifting	16
Embracing Definition	17
The Courage to Be Simple	17
The Right to Want	18
The Weight Of (Un)Fairness and the Path to Self-Alignment	19
Embodiment of Feelings	20
The Courage to Be Vulnerable	20
When You Feel Blamed	22
Moving Beyond "I Don't Know"	22
The Weight of Worry	23
Understanding Guilt	25
When Guilt Replaces Will	25
Speaking Without Shrinking	26
How to Use Anger Without Letting It Use You	27
Your Shadow Doesn't Need to Be Fixed, It Needs to Be Seen	28
The Illusion of Quick Fixes	29
Initiative Versus Reactivity: Choosing Your Influence	29

Confusion: When Old Truths Stop Working	30
The Right Time for Change	30
The In-Between of Change	31
The Quiet Pride That Keeps You from Contributing	32
Impatience	32
Outrage	32
Living Between Opposites	32
From Idea to Embodiment	33
The Trap of Being Mysterious	33
Stubbornness	34
Beyond Complaining	34
You Don't Have to Be So Serious	35
Outside Recognition	35
You Don't Earn Worthiness, You Remember It	35
Trauma and Its Relationship to Shame	36
Presence	36
Listening to What Wasn't Said	37
Changing by Remembering	37
Let the Words Find You	38
The Art of Talking	39
What Happened to Your Joy?	40
Craziness & Intuition: When Reality Feels Distorted	41
Walking Your Own Path	42
Chapter 2: Seeing with New Eyes	**43**
Growth Through Discomfort	43
On Being Normal	44
Choosing to Show Up	44
The Respect We Didn't Grow Up With	45
The Right to Take Responsibility	46
Stuckness	47
Hate Connects	47
Secrecy: Power, Not Just Shame	47
Practicing Alignment	48

Acceptance as Transcendence	48
Adulthood as an Ongoing Process of Maturation	48
The Limits of Integration	51
The Trap of Idealism	51
When Belonging Replaces Integrity	52
Harmony	53
On Truth in Relationships	53
The Simplicity of Hardship	54
Wisdom	54
Stop Trying to Change, That's When It Happens	54
Victimhood and Responsibility	55
Hope Isn't Naive, It's Necessary	56
The Fear and Relief of Being Seen	57
The Journey to Trustworthiness	57
The Grip of Fear	58
The Illusion of Being Special	59
Part II - Reflections on Family and Intimate Relationships	60
Introduction	60
Chapter 3: Healing Family Bonds	62
Understanding Yourself Through Your Past	62
Recognizing the Person Behind the Parent	63
Roots and Guidance: The Freedom that Comes from Clarity	63
Educating Our Children: A Mirror of Ourselves	64
Values Versus Boundaries: The Foundation of Meaningful Guidance	65
Hope for Our Children: Trusting Their Journey	66
The Importance We Hold as Parents	67
Chapter 4: The Threads Between Us	68
The Reciprocity of Giving and Receiving	68
Cultivating Skillfulness in Relationships	69
Connection Requires Effort	69
The Weight of Unfinished Business	70
Punishing Isolation	71

Boundaries Are Fluid	71
Honesty or Hidden Manipulation?	72
Making Room for More Than One Truth	73
The Need to Know Yourself	74
The Role of Compromise	74
Presence	75
The Challenge of Authenticity	75
The Difference Between Reaction and Action	76
The Complexity of Attachment	76
Freedom Through Truthfulness	77
The Search for Balance	77
The Pull of Drama	78
Connection Through Suffering	78
The Trap of Approval: Choosing Truth Over Being Liked	79
When Your Smile Isn't Honest	80
How Empathy Can Turn into Overextension	81
Beyond Emotional Highs: What Creates Real Depth	81
The Challenge of Recognizing and Expressing Needs	82
When Strength Becomes Isolation	84
To Choose Is to Be Seen	84
Turning Feeling into Form	85
Stop Waiting to Be Chosen	86
Always & Never: The Trap of Absolutes	86
Disappointment: A Mirror to Expectations	88
Chapter 5: Inside the Mystery of Love	**89**
The Many Faces of "I Love You"	90
The Power of Acknowledging Needing Another	90
The Reality of Unconditional Love	91
Drama and Passion	92
We Often Step into Roles That Make Us Resentful Later On	92
The Hidden Wounds Behind the Roles We Play	93
Trust Versus Safety: A Misunderstood Relationship	94
Meeting Your Partner Where They Are	95

Rewriting the Unspoken Rules of Partnership	96
The Power Play of Innocence and Selflessness	97
Care and Will: When Care Masks Disconnection from the Self	98
The Difficulty and Gift of Honoring the Masculine and Feminine in Your Partner	98
Sharing Expectations	100
When Love Turns into a Scorecard	100
The Feeling of Being in It Together	102
Fighting: A Necessary Release	104
Objectification: A Misunderstood Necessity	104
Sexual Desire: The Ebb and Flow of Intimacy	105
Desire and Love	105
The Battle, Who's the Better Sex?	106
The Weight of Words Between Women and Men	108
Taking Feedback	109
Codependency: Beyond the Negative Stigma	110
Commitment and the Fear of Losing Ourselves	110
Trust and Betrayal: Moving Beyond Fixed Roles	111
Flirting: The Unspoken Message	112
Making Our Partners Happy: A Power Lost	112
The Collective Side of Struggles	113
The Fear of Losing Yourself in Love	113
Wounds as Pathways to Growth	114
Necessary Lies	115
Your Partner Should Love and Accept Your Family	115
Love, Projection, and the Reality That Follows	116
Meeting Someone Who Can Carry Their Own Cross	117
The Highest Potential	117
The Ideal of Being Best Friends in Love	118
The Many Faces of Separation	118
Separation as a Path to Understanding	120
Divorce: When Projections Break but Nothing Rebuilds	121

Appendix A – Therapy: A Space for Reconnection   123
Appendix B – Further Reading   126

Dedication

For those seeking to stay close to what is true, as it is.

Preface

I was born and raised in Frankfurt, the third of four children, at a time when the Holocaust loomed large over the lives of Jews in postwar Germany. Questions about identity and inclusion formed part of the daily conversations that I heard from an early age. A central question, typical for many Jews around the world, but particularly accentuated for those in Germany, was this: *Am I a German Jew or a Jew living in Germany?*

Additional kinds of complexity and richness arose because my parents were immigrants from Iran and Syria. The complexity stemmed in part from the fact that, as an Oriental Jewish family, we weren't directly affected by the Shoah, but living as Jews still brought with it themes of safety and a sense of home. The richness came through an astonishing blend of cultures, I grew up hearing Farsi, Arabic, Hebrew, Italian, and German, all somehow seamlessly familiar, with each culture adding color through the food, traditions, and people it represented in my family. All in all, this diversity of experiences aroused in me a deep curiosity about belonging, identity, and the unseen forces that shape human lives.

As an adult, I spent years building a career in the corporate and business world as a strategy consultant, entrepreneur, and organizational advisor. On the surface, my life was fulfilling. Yet, beneath the sense of social and structural success, something felt misaligned, a quiet but persistent discomfort that grew harder to ignore. At 40, a milestone of transition in many traditions, I stepped away from everything familiar, drawn toward a deeper exploration of self. I remember this as a time filled with doubts, many question marks appeared before me concerning what it means to show up in life.

A counselor suggested that I take time out for a couple of days to be with myself in isolation. By that time, I had traveled extensively for business and pleasure, often on my own, but always toward a destination, project, or a place to join others. This time, I simply went into the desert. During the day, I sat alone for hours on a mattress, waiting. I made space for insights to come. I wrote a lot without any predefined questions. Already on the second day, something appeared with startling clarity and alignment; I wanted to become a counselor. This insight seemed only to deepen in the subsequent days, and it felt deeply liberating to finally connect with a desire that was truly mine.

What followed was a years-long period of self-reflection and intensive self-inquiry. This journey led me to uncover the layers of adaptation, survival strategies, and self-betrayal that had shaped my personality. Therapy, shadow work, and various group processes, including many encounter groups, became my gateway to something essential, an understanding that much of who we believe ourselves to be is a collection of past wounds and learned defenses. This journey soon led me to be not only a participant in but also a student of these various therapeutic methodologies. My intense love for this work manifested in realizing my dream of becoming a therapist in my own right.

My path was guided by renowned teachers such as Svagito Liebermeister and Rafia Morgan, alongside training in family constellations, somatic work, breathwork, polarity, and shadow integration. Beyond any methodology, what continues to fuel my work is a deep fascination with the contradictions and complexities of being human.

As a therapist and facilitator, my work centers on creating spaces of inquiry, healing, and integration. I believe that relationships, with their tensions, betrayals, and mirrors, offer the greatest opportunity for self-discovery. Through my private practice, I support individuals and couples in navigating the complexities of connection, self-awareness, and personal growth. A central aspect of this work is my role as a senior facilitator in the 7-day retreat called "Path of Love," which I've found to be the most beautiful and loving way to meet our shadows, befriend them, and feel more whole again. This sense of alignment allows for a profound meeting with our essence, enabling us to reach out to the world from that place. The Path of Love is the deepest, most transformational journey I myself have embarked on, and I've been honored to be a part of facilitating since 2015.

Writing has always been a way for me to translate experience into understanding. This book is part of that ongoing process, an exploration rather than a conclusion, a conversation rather than a doctrine. I approach life as a continuous unfolding, believing that the search for clarity is not about arriving at fixed truths but about staying open to what emerges.

Acknowledgments

This book is dedicated to my children, Joel, Noam, David, and Rhea. Being a parent has taught me a profound sense of meaningful responsibility that I could not have learned elsewhere. It has also helped me understand that no matter what I do or achieve in the outside world, nothing carries real relevance unless I can bring it into my family unit.

I want to acknowledge my first wife, Daniela, with whom I share the gift of my three sons. The journey of parenting together has been one of immense learning, shaping my understanding of love, responsibility, and commitment in ways I could never have anticipated.

My wife, Zhanna, has been a profound presence in my life for the past twelve years. Her love, intelligence, and insightful support have deeply influenced my personal and professional growth, helping me more fully become the person I'm meant to be.

My loving parents, Morris and Rachel, gave me everything they had, and I am deeply grateful for their love and support throughout my life. The path I've taken is deeply linked to what they gave me, what I misunderstood about their love, what they could not give, and, just as importantly, what I was not ready to receive.

I was fortunate to have shared the presence and wisdom of many teachers, and I want to mention two by name: Rafia Morgan and Svagito Liebermeister. Their love, at times tough but always real, challenged me and allowed me to grow in ways for which I am forever grateful.

Finally, I want to express my deepest gratitude to the many clients I have met over the past 20 years in my private practice and through the workshops

I have created and facilitated around the world. It is their trust in me that has allowed me to delve deeply into their life stories and explore the important themes outlined in this book.

Introduction - Embracing Life's Dualities: An Invitation

The intention of this book is to create clarity, evoke curiosity about your duality and complexity, and, above all, help you open your heart to embrace this duality. Clarity ultimately appears in those rare moments when one's personality is absent, but also through recognizing that much of what impacts you originates not from the outside, but from within, through accepting the layers of your inner complexity. Curiosity allows you to explore both your light and shadow. By delving into this duality, you open your heart to the vulnerability of being imperfect while still knowing you have the right to belong.

Life is rarely black or white. While good and bad, healthy and unhealthy exist, life also offers infinite shades of gray. Nuance reveals truth, while generalization often serves as a hiding place. For example, saying "He's incapable of being a good friend" is a broad judgment, but saying "He's not a good friend to me" makes it personal and helps you see what you need. A small step like this opens a door through which you can discover something about yourself. We often generalize to avoid getting lost in the details, yet it is in the details where we find our own story unfolding, a story of contradictions.

When our will is intact, it carries a quiet expectation that the world will help us bring it to life, that family, community, and institutions will stand behind us. But when our will is fractured through upbringing, we grow into adulthood already convinced that we are alone, that no one will stand with us. This early fracture makes even the simplest acts of self-expression feel unsafe because we no longer assume we will be supported.

In past generations, strong family, cultural, and religious ties provided a framework into which our will could extend and find its place. Today, those structures have weakened, and individualism has risen to fill the vacuum. While individual freedom can be a gift, it also leaves us with the daunting task of creating meaning and values on our own. This kind of individualism is often celebrated as liberation, yet such celebrations rarely acknowledge the weight of what has been lost or the difficulty of replacing it. Without roots, we may drift in the name of freedom, unaware of how much our will depends on feeling held by something larger than ourselves.

A part of today's hardship is rooted in this confusion. We have moved away from family and hierarchy into a culture of individualism. More than ever, this shift requires you to take responsibility for the expression of your own life in the ever-widening absence of guiding values or traditions. While in the past, through strong family, cultural, and religious ties, we were told which life choices were worthy or unworthy, you now face the challenge of determining what to be in service of, on your own.

A key theme of this book is the value of embracing limitations. Limitations, often seen as negative or something to avoid, are in fact essential for establishing meaning and purpose. Bert Hellinger aptly said, "There is no freedom without boundaries." What constrains us also provides structure, shapes our values, and lays the foundation for meaningful connection.

For example, a relationship is a limitation, it confines us to the interaction between two people and the needs, challenges, and vulnerabilities it evokes. Yet, this very confinement encourages us to delve deeply into the intricacies of our personality and how it meets the other. It pushes us to explore what truly matters to us, what we can offer, and where we seek nourishment. By embracing limitation in a constructive way, we open ourselves to the possibility of creating something uniquely meaningful, something that thrives within life's natural constraints.

This book does not offer direct solutions. It is not a roadmap or a self-help manual with "five steps to relaxation" or "how to have happy relationships." Instead, it is an invitation to view yourself as a continuous process of discovery,

INTRODUCTION - EMBRACING LIFE'S DUALITIES: AN INVITATION

one that is best served by staying curious about the many layers of experience. My intention is for this writing to serve as a reminder of life's complexity and of the humility and vulnerability needed to navigate it without falling into righteousness, judgmental comparison, or victimhood. It seeks to honor the "this and that" rather than the "this or that." Navigating these nuances requires intuition and courage, understanding that choices are necessary not for rigidity, but for movement and growth. I hope that reading this book provides moments of resonance and relaxation, even as it reveals difficulty or ignites resistance. Truth, no matter how unsettling, offers a sense of coming home.

This book invites you to sit with life's contradictions and complexities, to welcome them, and in doing so, to discover a deeper humanity and simplicity within yourself. It is designed as a companion to be explored intuitively, allowing you to follow what draws your attention rather than reading it from cover to cover. It seeks to inspire your intuitions. The topics are not definitive; you may view them through different lenses, and some themes naturally repeat or overlap. The intention is to leave space for you to explore your own perspectives and truths. Some reflections may seem obvious. If so, recognize the clarity you already possess, and move on to another theme.

The title of the book, The Courage to Be Simple, reflects what life ultimately asks of us: to meet it directly. Not with the sophistication, specialness, or collapse through which our personality often distances us from truth, but with the willingness to be real, honest, and to name things as they are. Simplicity is not naïveté. It is an intentional stance toward life's many curveballs, a refusal to complicate what can be met with clarity and presence. Our personality resists simplicity, but our longing to be real, close to our heart and essence, deeply desires it. This is where connection happens.

Defining and writing about these topics allows me to share what fascinates me in my work with individuals, couples, and groups. My many years of doing this work have helped me to see how themes are interconnected, coexisting while also contradicting one another. To preserve the essence of these complexities, I have chosen to capture them briefly rather than surround them with elaborate theories. This concise structure allows me to share insights without being bound by rigid formality, it serves my way of connecting the dots.

The book is divided into two parts. Part I - *Reflections on Personality and Life's Dualities*, explores our inner landscape with questions of awareness, authenticity, and the ongoing effort to integrate what has been relegated to the shadow. It includes *Finding the Self Beneath the Self* and *Seeing with New Eyes*, both of which examine the movements, tensions, and contradictions that shape our inner life.

Part II - *Reflections on Family and Intimate Relationships*, turns toward the relational field. It opens the themes of family in *Healing Family Bonds*, relationships in *The Threads Between Us*, and intimate partnership in *Inside the Mystery of Love*. Each section is followed by reflections and insights presented without specific order, encouraging an intuitive and personal exploration.

Part I - Reflections on Personality and Life's Dualities

Introduction

Life often challenges us to define who we are, both to ourselves and to others. These challenges, though inevitable, create friction within us and with the world around us. Much of this friction arises from our attempts to define ourselves, often through the identities we adopt or the roles we play. Definitions, however, are rarely fixed. They shift with our experiences, leaving us in a perpetual search for the right understanding of who we are. This ongoing endeavor, while disorienting at times, can also leave us feeling ungrounded and confused.

Yet within this uncertainty lies an opportunity. The process of figuring ourselves out invites us to uncover the layers of complexity beneath seemingly simple themes. Consider, for example, the concept of trust. At first glance, it may seem binary; we either trust or we do not. But upon closer examination, trust reveals a spectrum of nuances shaped by history, context, and vulnerability. Many other themes we navigate in life, though appearing one dimensional, carry hidden depth and richness.

A central difficulty emerges early in life, when we are conditioned to prioritize emotional survival. We instinctively seek belonging, recognition, and acceptance, often at the expense of our authentic selves. Yet the idea of the authentic self does not imply that a fully formed or capable part of us is ready from the beginning. Developing a personality, adopting values, and acquiring skills, even if some of these need to be unlearned later, are necessary steps in learning how to live. Still, within this process of adaptation, we often lose touch with an inherent and unique part of us that quietly seeks expression. This loss creates a subtle disconnection, even if we cannot immediately recognize it.

The discomfort of this disconnection often appears as an unsettling sense of duality or fakeness. Our natural traits and authentic parts become entangled with psychological complexes and wounds. This entanglement is shaped by conditioning that instills shame and guilt, slowly eroding our sense of authenticity and self-worth. Even so, a quiet knowing often remains within us, a sense that something deeper awaits and can bring us closer to feeling at home with ourselves.

As life unfolds through love, meaning, choices, betrayals, and other complexities, another challenge becomes clear. We often find ourselves caught between two powerful forces: freedom and belonging. Belonging to family, relationships, communities, or professional spheres requires compromise and the surrender of certain parts of ourselves. When this compromise becomes too heavy to bear, we retreat in search of freedom. Yet taken to an extreme, freedom can leave us isolated and alone, stripped of meaning. At the same time, it is often in isolation that we encounter our essence and explore our creativity. This ongoing struggle to balance freedom and connection is a deeply human challenge that tends to resurface throughout life with varying intensity.

Understanding ourselves also depends on the presence of awareness. Conscious inquiry, reflection, and experience allow awareness to bring hidden truths to light and foster integration. While often celebrated as a cornerstone of personal growth, awareness is sometimes misunderstood or overvalued in isolation. It can become indulgent, a way to inflate the ego or avoid the vulnerability needed to anchor ourselves in the dual nature of the human experience. True awareness requires courage: confronting the roles we play, accepting their costs, and facing our traumas without turning them into excuses. Awareness without humility risks leading to disconnection, but when it is paired with vulnerability, it becomes a transformative force that fosters genuine growth and deeper connection.

In this exploration, we eventually meet the parts of ourselves we would rather avoid. These include thoughts, impulses, and emotions that do not fit with who we believe we should be. C.G. Jung called this the shadow. It is made of traits we have learned to reject in ourselves, often because they were shamed, punished, or simply did not fit the roles we had to play in order to be accepted. Some limitations deserve their difficult reputation because they grow from what lies in the shadow: the unacknowledged and repressed aspects of ourselves shaped by past wounds and complexes. These hidden parts can create self-hatred and disconnection from ourselves and others. Although the shadow carries shame, guilt, and feelings of being undeserving of love or belonging, it is not something to transcend but to integrate. This integration is essential for fostering healthier relationships and rediscovering our humanity.

All of this returns us to a simple truth. Life, at its core, is about connection, having it, losing it, and regaining it with ourselves and with others. By embracing complexity, accepting limitations, and confronting our shadows, we can nurture the connections that make life meaningful and alive. This balance allows us to move beyond the need to be special and into a space of authenticity and shared humanity, where genuine growth and fulfillment can unfold. Ultimately, this book revolves around what enhances or blocks connection, not by seeking to transcend what makes us human but by embracing and including more and more of it.

Chapter 1: Finding the Self Beneath the Self

The way you see yourself is greatly shaped by the unconscious strategies you've carried for years. Beneath your habits and reactions live stories, wounds, and loyalties that influence how you love, work, and dream. This chapter invites you to look closely, not to judge or fix yourself, but to understand more about the roots of your patterns and the quiet truths that guide you. When you see yourself more clearly, you make space for change and greater choice, without losing your essence.

Understanding Begins with Accepting Limits

Healing often begins with understanding, but understanding is not a straightforward or purely intellectual process. It is layered, subtle, and often incomplete unless it includes a crucial component: the acceptance of limitations.

Take fire as an example. You may understand how it works, how to protect yourself from it and how to use it to your advantage. But that understanding only becomes useful when you also accept fire's limitations: that it can harm, and that caution and safety measures are non-negotiable.

The same is true when it comes to your past. You may come to understand your personal history, your wounds, your patterns, your family dynamics, but if you don't also accept the limitations it has imposed on your life, the insight remains hollow. Healing cannot take root if you are still clinging to

CHAPTER 1: FINDING THE SELF BENEATH THE SELF

the belief that things should have been different or that your past's effects on you will magically disappear. That wish keeps you stuck in resistance, rather than allowing you to move forward.

True understanding involves letting go of the fantasy of a different past and facing the reality of what was. This deeper acceptance doesn't come easily. It requires humility and a willingness to encounter one of the most difficult emotional states: helplessness. We are taught to avoid it and reject it at all costs. But paradoxically, it's in moments of surrender to this helplessness that the alchemy of healing can occur.

There is no clear roadmap for this journey. It unfolds slowly, often quietly, and sometimes painfully. But in those rare moments where understanding meets acceptance, where your insight allows you to soften into what is rather than fight what was, something profound can happen. It's in those moments that true transformation becomes possible.

The Limits That Make Freedom Real

Living in alignment with your values naturally places limits on your freedom, but those limits are not restrictions. They are the shape your freedom takes when it's guided by meaning. Without clear values, freedom can feel expansive on the surface but hollow underneath. In that emptiness, it's easy to chase after substitutes: spiritual trends, imagined ideals, or the fantasy of boundless choice.

When your values are unclear, your actions may stem more from self-justification than true exchange. You might find yourself taking, seeking affirmation, novelty, or validation, without truly offering yourself in return. But freedom without commitment, without a felt sense of responsibility, rarely leads to fulfillment. It leaves you drifting.

Obligation, when rooted in values, isn't a burden. It's what creates structure, reciprocity, and depth in your relationships and commitments. It anchors you. And though it limits certain choices, it also makes others deeply meaningful.

In the end, it's not freedom from limits we long for, but freedom within them. The kind that emerges when your choices are shaped by what you truly stand for.

Perspectives Keep on Shifting

Life is an unfolding journey, marked by stages where you may feel a sense of "arrival" or certainty, only to be upended by new insights or experiences. At every stage, you seek engagement and aliveness, but it's crucial to recognize that these feelings manifest differently over time. What excites or engages you in a particular moment is not an ultimate truth but a reflection of your needs and understanding at that time, a temporary station to be lived and appreciated.

Enthusiasm can sometimes harden into ideology, however, when you cling to a particular phase or passion, treating it as the only valid path. A new philosophy, way of life, or meaningful project may initially bring excitement and purpose, but if you begin to believe it must apply universally or indefinitely, rigidity sets in. This often shows up as self-righteousness, a need to persuade others, or frustration when people don't share your perspective.

The joy of discovery can shift into the pressure of maintaining or defending the identity you've built around it. Recognizing when enthusiasm has hardened into ideology is essential for growth. The key is to stay present with excitement without over-identifying with it, allowing for the expression of your freedom to evolve. Life continuously presents new stages, each bringing changes that challenge and enrich you.

Your readiness for these transitions is best expressed by recognizing and accepting them as natural parts of life's flow. By honoring the aliveness you feel in each moment without turning it into a fixed narrative, you leave space for new experiences and perspectives to shape you, keeping you open to life's ongoing evolution.

Embracing Definition

There is often a fear of being defined or seen as definable by others, as it feels like a limitation on your freedom to change and evolve, or even diminishes your sense of "specialness." To avoid this, you may prefer to keep things vague and undefined. Yet, allowing yourself to be defined and acknowledged in a specific way can deepen your experience and understanding of who you are. Over time, when change is necessary, it will arise naturally, enabling you to expand or transition into a new form of self-expression.

It is your responsibility to cultivate the strength to stand firmly in your current identity while also having the courage to let it go when it no longer aligns with your inner truth. Being defined does not mean being trapped; rather, it provides a foundation from which growth and transformation can emerge.

The Courage to Be Simple

Simplicity isn't about doing less or lowering your standards, it's about dropping what's performative and returning to what's real. At its heart, simplicity is a form of honesty. It asks you to show up without strategy, without comparison, without the need to be impressive.

This kind of honesty is vulnerable. It means letting go of the stories you tell to appear humble or the quiet self-criticism you use to avoid deeper reflection. It means being willing to see yourself clearly, your strengths and your limits, without needing to fix, perform, or justify.

Letting go through simplicity is an invitation: to stop performing, and start being.

The Right to Want

Your will is the inner force that says: I want, I choose, I'm here. It gives shape to your individuality and provides a sense of orientation and relevance in the world. But for many, that will is fractured early in life, muted by shame, fear, or the subtle conditioning that it's safer to comply than to assert.

Over time, this disruption blurs the line between what you truly want and what you believe you're supposed to want. The expectations of others, parents, teachers, partners, even broad cultural norms, begin to speak louder than your own voice. And slowly, your choices no longer feel like your own.

When your will is fractured, you might become externally highly adaptable but inwardly disconnected. You may hesitate before acting, defer to others' desires, or find yourself paralyzed by seemingly simple decisions. Reclaiming your will isn't just about being more decisive, it's about coming home to yourself.

Practice: Begin by noticing how you speak about your desires. Try completing simple sentences like:

- I want...
- I won't...
- I choose...

Observe what arises in your body as you say them. Do they feel true? Do they bring up guilt, fear, or resistance? This simple act of naming your will can begin to restore the connection to your inner voice. Over time, you may find it easier to act from alignment rather than expectation.

Reclaiming your will is not a declaration of selfishness. It's an act of integration. It allows you to move through life not from habit or fear but from clarity, choice, and a quiet sense of inner authority.

CHAPTER 1: FINDING THE SELF BENEATH THE SELF

The Weight Of (Un)Fairness and the Path to Self-Alignment

When someone habitually views life through the prism of (un)fairness, that often signals the presence of a deeper story rooted in childhood. It speaks of moments when we felt helpless and alone as the target or bystander to ruthlessness, violence, or the mistreatment of those close to us, situations where we were powerless or ineffective in responding.

These early experiences of powerlessness and resulting rage can leave you with a deep desire to restore fairness and ensure justice, a desire you carry into adulthood. This often manifests in efforts to promote civility, teach manners to others, or advocate for marginalized groups you perceive as helpless. Beneath this helplessness often lies your own rage, a profound anger directed at those who hold or held power.

When fairness and unfairness, or justice and injustice, becomes your dominant lens, it can leave you feeling trapped in endless advocacy, neglecting your own wounds or needs in the present. In your efforts to interpret and meet the needs of others, you hope to reclaim a sense of potency and agency. Over time, righteousness and rigid adherence to principles can overshadow a deeper understanding of what truly matters to you and what you genuinely need in any given moment.

Practice: Shift your focus inward. Instead of fixating on external (un)fairness or representing higher ideals, sense what it would feel like to simply represent yourself. This involves reconnecting with your own sense of right and wrong, acknowledging what feels comfortable or uncomfortable, and re-establishing your boundaries. This practice may feel ordinary and unremarkable, but it is challenging as you are shifting the focus from the extraordinary (outside) to the ordinary (yourself). A painful loss of identity may follow.

By redirecting your attention inward repeatedly over time, you regain balance. This shift allows you to meet your own needs and make choices that are more aligned with your true sense of self. As you move away from a constant focus on external (un)fairness, you cultivate a deeper, more grounded connection to yourself, enabling you to navigate life with greater clarity and integrity.

Embodiment of Feelings

To embody a feeling, especially pain or hurt, is to enter into direct contact with your limits. These moments can be overwhelming, as a single emotion often takes up all the space inside you, eclipsing access to other parts of yourself. Because of this intensity, many people prefer to stay at the surface, where emotions can be observed or spoken about but not actually felt.

For example, you might say, "I'm distrustful," believing you're naming a real emotion. But have you truly felt what that distrust feels like inside you, how it shapes your body, your breath, and your relationships? Or are you subtly shifting the focus outward, implying that others are untrustworthy while avoiding the discomfort of owning your vulnerability?

Embodiment means feeling the weight and consequence of your emotions, understanding how something like distrust has shaped your worldview, your choices, and your sense of safety. When you allow yourself to feel that fully, without flinching or deflecting blame, something shifts. You begin to reclaim responsibility for your inner life. From this place, alignment becomes possible, not by changing the world around you, but by facing yourself with honesty and compassion.

The Courage to Be Vulnerable

Vulnerability is how you tap into your humanity and connect with others, and yourself, on a deeper level. But true vulnerability requires a solid inner foundation: a self strong enough to hold your light and shadow, strengths and limitations, successes and flaws without collapsing.

At its essence, vulnerability is about being real, honestly naming what you feel, need, and fear, without manipulating, guilt-tripping, or falling into self-victimization. When you're rooted in a stable sense of self, this kind of honesty becomes possible, not because it's easy, but because you're no longer defined by the reactions it may provoke, and because the betrayal of your own integrity becomes too painful to bear.

CHAPTER 1: FINDING THE SELF BENEATH THE SELF

From this place, vulnerability invites you to express your needs and desires openly. But this is often where the challenge lies. Many people have distanced themselves from clearly expressing, or even knowing, their needs, relying instead on roles, unspoken contracts, and ideologies to navigate relationships. Vulnerability asks you to move beyond these defenses, to risk being seen as you are (with your duality and contradictions), and to accept the possibility that your needs may go unmet.

Many natural human needs, such as alone time, curiosity, touch, belonging, safety, and meaning, become sources of embarrassment due to past experiences, leaving you disconnected from your true self. Instead of asking for what you need, you may resort to taking, manipulating, or controlling. True vulnerability also requires you to confront the limitations inherent in being human. It is not about making grand statements or seeking pity but about finding the courage to, for example, say, "I need you," and mean it. This can feel daunting because vulnerability demands that you let go of your self-importance and embrace the simplicity of being ordinary. It asks you to prioritize connection over righteousness and to accept the dualities that make you human.

Vulnerability also has a dark side that warrants exploration. It can be misused as a tool for control, manipulation, or moral superiority. Behaviors such as dramatizing emotions, blackmailing through sadness or silence, or using vulnerability to assert power over others are distortions that disconnect you. Authentic vulnerability, by contrast, is free of strategy. It is not about leveraging your needs to gain something but about owning them as part of who you are.

It requires you to make peace with not always knowing what you want or need and to stay open to discovering those truths as you expose yourself to others. Vulnerability teaches you to live with contradictions and unanswered questions, helping you embrace your humanity with greater authenticity. Ultimately, vulnerability is the courage to connect without pretense. It asks you to release your attachment to outcomes and to trust in the process of gradually understanding. In doing so, it opens pathways to intimacy and self-awareness, reminding you that connection, not perfection, is the most profound expression of your humanity.

When You Feel Blamed

When you feel blamed or criticized, it can instantly transport you to feelings of rejection, shame, or inadequacy you first knew in childhood. In those moments, your body reacts before your mind can process: you rush to explain, to defend, to justify. This reaction is natural. It's a survival reflex, shaped by years of needing to protect yourself from judgment or pain.

But while this instinct may once have kept you safe, it can now prevent you from hearing what's actually being said, or feeling what's really going on inside you. The drive to excuse yourself often overrides the deeper work: noticing your vulnerability, understanding your emotional patterns, and responding with presence instead of protection.

Practice: The next time you feel that tightening in your chest, that urge to interrupt or defend, pause. Take a breath. Ask yourself gently: What am I trying not to feel? What am I afraid might be true? In this quiet space, you might uncover something raw: a need for love, a fear of failure, or an old story you still carry.

By staying present with your discomfort rather than reacting from it, you begin to see your survival patterns for what they are: intelligent but outdated. And with that awareness, you can begin to relate, not react. You open the door to deeper self-trust and more meaningful connections with others. Notice and resist the impulse to "excuse yourself."

Moving Beyond "I Don't Know"

Our words are often more powerful than we realize. They can serve as bridges to truth, or as barriers that keep us safe from what we're not ready to face. Take the phrase, "I don't know."

In conversation, especially with people close to us, "I don't know" can become a habitual response to discomfort.

- "Why are you upset?" "I don't know."
- "Do you want to stay or leave?" "I don't know."

It sounds honest. Sometimes, it is. But often, it's a shield, a way to avoid what we know but don't want to name. We say it when we're afraid to confront what we feel, what we want, or what needs to change. Beneath the surface of "I don't know," there is often something clear, but vulnerable. Naming it might risk rejection, responsibility, or relational shifts we're not ready for.

Growth begins when we stop hiding behind uncertainty. When we pause and ask ourselves: *If I did know, what might the answer be? What am I afraid to say out loud?*

Practice: The next time you catch yourself about to say "I don't know," pause. Ask:

- Am I protecting myself from something?
- What am I afraid might happen if I spoke honestly?
- Is there a small piece of truth I'm willing to explore?

You don't have to force clarity, but you can create space for honesty. Even saying, "I'm scared to say" or "I have to think about it" is more connecting than "I don't know." That's where real dialogue begins.

The Weight of Worry

Worry is often mistaken for love. We tell ourselves that worrying about someone means we care for them, that it's an expression of devotion or connection. But when you look more closely, worry reveals something more complicated.

At times, worrying about someone carries an unspoken message: *I don't trust you to handle your life.* It can slip into control disguised as care.

Other times, worry keeps you busy, fixated on the struggles of others, so you don't have to face your own fears, helplessness, or vulnerability. It creates the illusion that if you just think hard enough, plan carefully enough, and anticipate every possibility, you might keep suffering at bay. But worry doesn't protect you. It traps you. It freezes the energy that would otherwise move you forward, into connection, into excitement, into life.

Worry also masquerades as responsibility. It keeps you circling without ever landing on a clear commitment. When you worry, you feel involved, but you haven't actually said what you're willing to take on, by when, or how. Real responsibility is explicit: I'll do this. I'll be there. Worry is diffuse; it protects you from the risk of failing at something specific by keeping everything general. It soothes the conscience without carrying the weight. Naming responsibility turns fear into action, and makes care tangible.

For those who live in constant worry, excitement becomes almost unrecognizable. Excitement pulls you toward possibility. Worry traps you in prediction. Both create energy, but only one leads you somewhere new.

And for those on the receiving end of your worry, the weight can be heavy. No matter how much they reassure you, they still feel your fear in the room. They feel the mistrust. They carry the invisible burden of trying to calm the part of you that doesn't believe they can survive without your worry.

Understanding the difference between care and worry doesn't mean you stop caring; it means you can begin offering your care in ways that free both you and the people you love, allowing life to move again.

Practice: Notice today when you slip into worry about someone. Instead of asking, "How can I protect them?" ask, "How can I trust them, and myself, more at this moment?"

And when you feel worry rising, ask a second question: "What am I actually willing to take responsibility for here?"

Understanding Guilt

Guilt is a reminder of misaligned choices and is often an unavoidable part of your existence, arising as a response to actions that conflict with accepted family or cultural values and norms. It is neither inherently good nor bad, but it becomes problematic when carried disproportionately, dominating your inner world and distorting your sense of self. Guilt often acts as a lens through which you view yourself and your relationships, keeping you preoccupied with your perceived failings. Paradoxically, this overemphasis on guilt inflates your sense of importance, as you become consumed by self-focused narratives rather than seeking genuine resolution. This cycle is perpetuated by a lack of clarity about what truly matters to you.

Guilt thrives on assumptions about what is important to others, leaving you disconnected from your own values and priorities. The clearer you become about what feels right and meaningful for you, the less guilt will dictate your every move. But keep in mind that stepping onto your own path may trigger the very feelings you wish to avoid, guilt and the fear of disappointing others.

When you examine the roots of your guilt, it can reveal lessons that transform it from a burden into a tool for growth and understanding.

When Guilt Replaces Will

When guilt becomes a frequent motivator for your actions, it can serve as an important wake-up call indicating that you are disconnected from your will, your inner source of direction and choice.

If you often feel guilty for coming home late, for not doing enough around the house, or for neglecting things you think you should be doing, it may not be about failing others at all. Instead, it points to a deeper disconnection from what you truly want to do.

In these moments, guilt functions as a substitute for will. It directs your attention outward, toward expectations you believe you must meet, while obscuring the simple truth that your heart is no longer aligned with what you're doing.

For example, feeling guilty about staying late at work may not mean you should try harder to balance things. It might mean that the work itself no longer serves you. The guilt, in that sense, is not punishment but information, a sign that you are acting against your own inner truth.

Practice: Notice when guilt arises in your daily life. Ask yourself: What would I actually want to do here if guilt wasn't guiding me? Explore whether guilt is covering for a lack of alignment between your actions and your authentic will.

Speaking Without Shrinking

In social settings, many people hide their strength, not because they lack clarity but because they fear the cost of expressing it. You may know what you think or feel, yet hold back from speaking directly. Instead, you soften your voice, add disclaimers, or downplay your certainty to avoid seeming arrogant, intense, or "too much."

Phrases like, "I'm not sure, but . . ." or "This might sound crazy . . ." become protective habits, ways of shrinking your presence so others won't feel threatened. These small hesitations often stem from earlier experiences where strength was met with shame, rejection, or discomfort in others. You learned it was safer to soften.

Even your body may play along, smiling when you don't mean to, using a lighter tone than what you feel inside. But that smile, that softened voice, becomes a mask that distances you from your truth.

Practice: Begin noticing when you dilute your clarity. Instead of rushing to buffer your words, pause. Feel your feet on the ground. Let your voice come from your body, not just your mind. Practice saying what you see, feel, or know, without apology. Not with aggression, but with presence.

CHAPTER 1: FINDING THE SELF BENEATH THE SELF

How to Use Anger Without Letting It Use You

Anger is one of the most misunderstood emotions. We're often taught to fear it, suppress it, or explode with it, but rarely to listen to it. At its core, anger is a messenger. It says: Something hurts. Something feels unfair. A boundary has been crossed.

Beneath anger, there's often a deeper plea: See me. Hear me. Don't humiliate or dismiss me. But when that plea feels too vulnerable, or when it's been ignored too many times, anger can harden into something else like sarcasm, silence, over-giving, withdrawal, or control. These are often learned defenses, shaped by early experiences of being shamed or punished for expressing frustration. They reflect a deeper discomfort with expressing needs directly.

When we grow up in environments where expressing anger led to rejection or conflict, we may carry a belief that our needs are dangerous, or that they'll only be met if we suppress or demand them. This can lead to a pattern of distorted expressions: aggression, passive-aggression, or avoidance. These strategies often create distance or escalate conflict without addressing what's really going on underneath.

To transform your relationship with anger, it's important to distinguish between its healthy and unhealthy forms:

- Distorted anger manipulates, controls, or defends. It's reactionary and disconnecting.
- Clear, assertive anger is grounded and honest. It says: *This matters to me. I want to be taken seriously.* It draws boundaries without cutting people off.

It's also important to recognize the difference between anger and rage. Assertive anger can clear the air and even build trust. Rage, on the other hand, seeks to punish or destroy. It often stems from older wounds that overwhelm your capacity to stay present. Anger says, *I feel this.* Rage says, *You are bad.*

The shift begins with awareness. When you feel anger rising, ask yourself:

- Am I trying to communicate, or to control?
- Am I naming my feelings, or attacking someone else's?
- Am I staying in the present, or reacting from old pain?

True strength lies not in suppressing anger or unleashing it, but in staying with it, just a moment longer, long enough to ask what it's really trying to show you.

Your Shadow Doesn't Need to Be Fixed, It Needs to Be Seen

The shadow isn't only made of what's "bad." It also contains vitality, creativity, and truth we've buried to protect ourselves. When we deny these parts, they don't disappear, they work underground. They show up in projections, in harsh judgments of others, or in the ways we quietly sabotage our relationships.

As long as you avoid looking at your darker sides, you stay trapped inside the image you're trying to protect, never fully honest about who you really are. Facing your shadow isn't about balancing light and dark like two sides of a scale. It's about letting go of the need to seem balanced at all. It's messy. It's uncomfortable. Sometimes, it feels like losing control of the story you tell about yourself.

Owning your dark side isn't about indulging it or using it as an excuse for harm. It's about meeting these disowned parts with honesty and curiosity, so they no longer control you from the shadows. In relationships, this means taking responsibility for your triggers and recognizing when you're reacting to the present, or to the past.

Shadow work isn't meant to feel comfortable. It's meant to make you real. And from that realness comes a kind of quiet strength, a trustworthiness that you can feel inside yourself and that others can feel too. Paradoxically, it's by embracing what feels least lovable in yourself that deeper intimacy becomes possible.

CHAPTER 1: FINDING THE SELF BENEATH THE SELF

The Illusion of Quick Fixes

Media is filled with promises and methods leading to a desired outcome. The "5 steps to happiness" or the "10 keys to a good marriage," and the list goes on to finding fulfillment and similar ideals. While these seem helpful, offering hope for change and inspiration through new perspectives, they often fail to support you on the path to genuine self-knowledge or self-esteem.

They dismiss the deeper nature of your wounds and perpetuate the illusion of an attainable, continuous state of happiness or strength. In doing so, they betray the depth you long for, bypassing the authentic inquiry that allows you to connect with your complexity and truth. It betrays and trivializes struggle in favor of superficial solutions.

Whenever there is a strong pull to follow a step-by-step process that promises resolution or transcendence of an inner struggle, it is worth asking: Where is there a betrayal of your depth and the inherent need for wholeness? Where is there resistance to listening to your intuition and recognizing what feels right or wrong?

Initiative Versus Reactivity: Choosing Your Influence

It's valuable to understand how we exert influence in life. Often, we find ourselves either taking initiative or reacting to what is being offered. Initiative stems from a sense of agency, the belief that we have the right to influence outcomes. In contrast, reactivity comes from seeking permission or waiting to be granted the opportunity to contribute.

When you take initiative, you actively shape the outcome you desire. Reactivity, on the other hand, involves joining others' initiatives and adapting to the framework someone else has established. Do you find yourself waiting for permission, or do you trust your right to influence the course of events?

Understanding whether you lean toward initiative or reactivity can clarify your natural tendencies and reduce inner conflict. It allows you to accept and work with your strengths rather than feeling burdened by unfairness ("Why is it always me who initiates?") or self-doubt ("I don't have the courage to initiate myself").

Confusion: When Old Truths Stop Working

Confusion pulls the ground out from under you, leaving you feeling disoriented, even threatened. Although it may feel like being stuck in the fog, confusion isn't a failure of clarity, it's a sign that something inside you is shifting. Often, it means that an old way of seeing no longer fits, but the new perspective hasn't arrived yet.

We tend to rush to fix confusion, to push it away or cover it with answers that feel safe. But if you pause instead, if you listen to the silence beneath the thought I don't know, you might notice that confusion is doing something important. It's softening rigid knowing. It's asking better questions. It's preparing space for a deeper truth to emerge.

Practice: The next time you feel confused, resist the urge to collapse into frustration or quick answers. Ask gently: *What part of me is being asked to grow? What assumptions no longer feel true?* Stay in the space between. That's often where transformation begins.

The Right Time for Change

We're not ready until we are. In hindsight, it's often difficult to understand why certain changes couldn't have been made earlier. Even when you've thought deeply, talked extensively, and intellectually understood the need for change, it may still fail to manifest in your life.

However, change doesn't occur until you feel its necessity, not just think it. True readiness arises only when an existential urgency becomes great enough to override the barriers holding you back. Your basic need for belonging, fear of exclusion, inability to fully embrace truth, and the courage required to face life's limitations all play significant roles in shaping your readiness for transformation.

Readiness is far from just being about intellectual understanding; it's about an alignment of circumstances, emotions, and will. Many factors must come together before you're truly prepared to move forward.

The In-Between of Change

Change often begins with disruption. It might arrive through heartbreak, depression, job loss, aging, or the quiet realization that you've outgrown something you once believed in. Whether triggered from within or forced by circumstance, change pushes you to let go of the familiar before you've fully stepped into the new.

In this in-between space, you may feel disoriented, like you've boarded a train that's already left the station, but you don't know where it's headed. There's no clear destination, no firm ground to stand on. Just movement, uncertainty, and the unsettling sense of not being who you once were . . . but not yet knowing who you're becoming.

And yet, even here, there are signs.

Look out the window. What's shifting in the landscape of your life? Have certain friendships become more important? Are different books, ideas, or people catching your attention? What decisions have you made recently that felt quiet, but meaningful?

These small changes are not random. They're signals. Signposts. Clues that something new is forming, guiding you, subtly, steadily, toward a deeper alignment with yourself.

The discomfort of change is real. But so is its wisdom.

The Quiet Pride That Keeps You from Contributing

A subtle form of self-centered perfectionism emerges when you believe you have nothing impactful to offer the world. This mindset can justify withholding your participation and contributions. The idea that what you give must be extraordinary, or only valuable if it has a significant impact, is, in itself, a trap. It quietly inflates your own importance and keeps you from engaging with life as you are.

Impatience

Impatience is a form of anxiety that whispers, "You don't have enough time," "No one will wait for you," or "You must do as much as possible to feel accomplished." It reflects an inner restlessness, fueled by a fear of inadequacy and an underlying pressure to prove your worth through constant action.

Outrage

When outrage becomes a habitual response to events in your life, it often signals an overreaction. This may point to a lower resilience to discomfort or an increased fear of being attacked. At its core, habitual outrage can also reflect a deep fear of not being seen or valued, an attempt to assert importance or demand attention through dramatic expressions of indignation.

Living Between Opposites

Life is shaped by opposites, freedom and responsibility, closeness and space, certainty and doubt. These tensions are not problems to be solved but rhythms to be lived. In accepting both, we find a steadier way to move through the world.

From Idea to Embodiment

Insight often begins as an idea, something that clicks in the mind, a concept that feels exciting, full of possibility. This stage can be intoxicating, but it is not yet transformation. True change only begins when insight travels from the head into the body, when it becomes an embodied experience.

Ideas live in the boundless realm of possibility; embodiment lives in the reality of limitation and truth. Some feelings cannot be changed; they can only be carried with dignity. And yet, this acceptance brings us closer to our essence. It is here, where our bodies remember and hold what is true, that we find the kind of alignment no concept can fully deliver.

The Trap of Being Mysterious

When someone can't be "figured out," it's often not true depth but a defense, one shaped early in life to stay safe by revealing little. Mystery becomes a way to attract others while keeping our real feelings hidden. Over time, we can get lost in this self-created riddle, adapting like a chameleon and mistaking concealment for connection.

Behind the veil of mystery often lies a deep fear of inadequacy. The performance of being unknowable becomes a substitute for authenticity, offering others the lure of a hidden jewel to be uncovered.

Liberation begins when we give up the need to be mysterious. In choosing openness over obscurity, we step back into simplicity, where being seen for who we are matters more than being admired for what others imagine us to be.

Stubbornness

At its core, stubbornness is often rooted in a deep fear of humiliation and a resistance to being seen as wrong. It's less about rejecting input and more about protecting a fragile sense of self-worth. Beneath the refusal to yield is often a quiet fear: If I'm wrong, I'm unlovable. If I yield, I disappear.

To truly address stubbornness, you have to meet the shame that fuels it. Letting that shame rise to the surface, without judgment, can begin to soften the defensive grip. This isn't about forcing yourself to agree or surrender but about creating enough safety to stay open when your instinct is to shut down.

Normalizing shame as a human experience rather than a personal failure makes room for flexibility, curiosity, and growth. Over time, the need to protect your worth through rigidity begins to loosen, allowing you to engage in dialogue without the fear that your value is on the line.

Beyond Complaining

As long as we move through life, or our relationships, as the dissatisfied who complain, we block our own maturation. Complaining is easy, but it places us in a posture of waiting, hoping that someone else will notice, fix, or soothe our discomfort.

This can turn into a never-ending cycle, fueled by the grip of victim energy. As long as we fail to recognize that whatever we dislike requires our responsibility, we continue to complain and project our problems outward. Complaining keeps us tethered to the illusion that relief will come from the outside, rather than from our own courage to act. It is worth asking: *Does this apply to me?*

Humility and maturity emerge when we shift from complaint to speaking clearly about what we want and need, expressing our expectations, and being ready to face the possibility that those needs might not be met. In this important shift, we reclaim our agency.

CHAPTER 1: FINDING THE SELF BENEATH THE SELF

You Don't Have to Be So Serious

Some people carry themselves with a kind of heaviness, mistaking seriousness for depth. But seriousness isn't always about being grounded or thoughtful. It can be a mask, a way of signaling importance while avoiding vulnerability. In this form, seriousness becomes self-centered, focused on how you're perceived rather than on what you truly care about.

Sincerity, by contrast, doesn't try to impress. It's not concerned with appearing wise or important. Instead, it's about showing up honestly, speaking from the heart, and allowing yourself to be seen without pretense. Sincerity is light, not because it's superficial, but because it's free of self-protection. It's the tone of someone genuinely trying to connect.

Where seriousness creates distance, making others feel they have to walk carefully, sincerity creates space. It says, "This is what matters to me. I'm here. I care." In relationships, in work, in art, sincerity opens the door to something real. Choosing it means being willing to be felt, not just understood.

Outside Recognition

When you rely heavily on external recognition, you betray yourself and pay the price of mediocrity. This dependency prevents you from discovering or pursuing your own unique path, leaving you disconnected from the road you need to travel.

You Don't Earn Worthiness, You Remember It

At the root of most psychological struggles in life is a quiet, painful belief: I don't matter enough. This sense of unworthiness doesn't always shout. Sometimes, it whispers. It shows up in hesitation, perfectionism, and staying silent when you long to speak.

Many people wait to feel worthy before they step into life fully, before they risk, contribute, create, and connect. But the paradox is: you don't feel your worth first. You build it by moving anyway.

You reclaim your worth not by trying to "become someone" worthy of living, but by participating, imperfectly, vulnerably, actively. It's in offering what you have, exactly as you are today, that you begin to stitch together the fabric of belonging.

Healing doesn't happen by thinking your way into self-esteem. It happens when you allow yourself to belong to life: to take up space, to bring your voice, to make mistakes, to give what's yours to give, even when the old fears still rattle.

Practice: Today, do one small thing that you would normally hesitate to do because you doubt yourself. It could be speaking up in a conversation, sharing something you created, or simply asking for help. Don't wait to feel ready. Move while still feeling uncertain.

Trauma and Its Relationship to Shame

Shame is one of the most pervasive obstacles to healing trauma. It stems from the belief that you should have fought harder, responded better, or been stronger and more resilient, that you somehow failed to prevent the event that caused the trauma. This self-blame compounds the trauma's impact on both your body and self-esteem. To address trauma, you must normalize shame, recognizing it as a natural response rather than a reflection of your worth or capability.

Presence

When you have a soulful, deep conversation, there's an intensity and quietness to it. The same exists with a soulful connection to anything, a person, the sun, or a cup of tea. These moments remind you of the depth and richness life holds when you are fully present. To be present, you have to know and feel that you're in the right place.

Listening to What Wasn't Said

Sometimes someone says all the right things, but something in you tenses. The words sound kind, reasonable, or honest, but your body feels off. Confused. Slightly guarded. This is the moment where listening goes beyond language.

Most of us are taught to listen politely, to take people at their word. But not everything spoken is clear or clean. Fear, power dynamics, self-deception, or emotional unawareness can distort what's being said, even with good intentions. Responsibility in communication isn't just about speaking clearly; it's also about listening with discernment.

You have the right to trust what resonates in you. To notice when something feels off, even if you can't explain it yet. Sometimes the truth comes in sensations before it comes in words. Your job isn't to accuse or withdraw, but to stay curious. Ask questions. Feel into what's being said and what isn't.

This is what it means to listen with both your mind and your intuition, not just to the other person, but to yourself. In doing so, you build not only more honest connections but also a deeper sense of trust in your own perception.

Changing by Remembering

At many points in life, you'll ask yourself the same quiet question: *What needs to change in me?* You search for more integration, more openness, less suffering. You want to evolve.

But often, the idea of change carries a hidden judgment, that something about you is wrong, broken, or not enough. And from that harsh place, real change becomes difficult. You try to force transformation by fixing, improving, correcting. It can feel like trying to love yourself with a clenched fist.

What if, instead of asking, *what needs to be fixed,* you asked, *what wants to be remembered?*

This question softens everything. It doesn't deny your longing for growth. It simply reframes it. Remembering suggests that the qualities you seek, compassion, clarity, courage, already exist within you. Maybe they were lost, buried, or never given space to grow. But they're not foreign. They belong to you.

For example, you might notice: "I struggle to respect the opposite sex, yet I long for a healthy relationship." It's hard to respect something you were never taught to see with nuance. But if you shift your view and say, "I remember my father's or mother's humanity, even their imperfections," something begins to open. You reconnect to a thread of respect that was always there, waiting to be acknowledged.

Practice: Instead of reaching for what's missing, pause and ask: What if I already have this, somewhere in me? What part of me is trying to return, not arrive for the first time?

Remembering reconnects you to your humanity. It's an act of inclusion, not correction. And in that space of reconnection, change happens more naturally. You begin to shift not because you're unworthy as you are, but because something in you is ready to come forward again.

You are not here to fix yourself like a broken object. You're here to keep returning, again and again, to the parts of you you've forgotten and to welcome them home.

Let the Words Find You

Words can bridge the gap between your inner world and someone else's understanding. But they often arrive imperfect, incomplete, or tangled. You may worry they'll fail you, that if you don't plan carefully, you'll say the wrong thing, reveal too much, or lose control.

And yet, these very moments, when you're unsure, exposed, or emotionally charged, are the ones that most need your truth. Not the polished version, but the raw, unfolding one.

When you feel vulnerable or angry, your instinct might be to retreat and script what you'll say. You shape the conversation in your mind, preparing arguments or soft landings. But this controlled speech rarely brings you closer to what really needs to be expressed. It may keep you safe, but it also keeps you stuck.

Practice: Try beginning to speak without knowing exactly what you'll say. Let the words come, even if they feel messy or uncertain. Speak slowly. Listen as you speak, not just to the other, but to yourself. You may be surprised by what rises to the surface: feelings you hadn't named, truths you hadn't known you were holding.

Speaking without a script isn't recklessness. It's trust. It's choosing connection over control. And when you allow your words to come from presence rather than performance, they become something more than communication, they become discovery. For both you and the person listening.

The Art of Talking

Talking about yourself is a skill, one that many of us never truly learn. We know how to explain, vent, and make a point. But often, we speak just to be understood, not to understand ourselves.

When you share your experience from a place of full identification, where the story is fixed and the emotion is absolute, there's little space for reflection or discovery. You're focused on what happened or how you feel but not on what your words might reveal to you in real time.

What changes everything is curiosity. When you slow down enough to feel what's happening as you speak, your thoughts, your reactions, your tone, you begin to access something deeper. Your words aren't just a report; they become a mirror. You start to notice what's true beneath the surface, what you didn't know you were holding, and how your story might be evolving.

This kind of speaking requires a pause. A breath. A willingness to let your logic and intuition speak together. It's slower, yes, but richer. More honest. And when you speak from that place, you not only connect more deeply with others, you reconnect with yourself.

What Happened to Your Joy?

Excitement is one of the most alive feelings we can experience. It connects you to wonder, curiosity, and the energy of possibility. At its core, excitement is spontaneous, childlike, vibrant, unfiltered. It doesn't ask for permission; it just rises.

But for many of us, that natural energy didn't remain untouched. As children, we may have been told to "calm down," "stop showing off," or "act more mature." We learned that our joy was too loud or too much. Over time, excitement became something to manage, not express freely.

For some families, a child's unfiltered enthusiasm felt threatening, like it exposed the family to judgment. And so, we quieted down. We toned it down, sometimes even to the point that we couldn't quite find it anymore.

As adults, that once-vital energy often feels distant. When others express excitement, we may find ourselves judging it, or feeling strangely irritated by it. What we're actually reacting to is our own disconnection from that part of ourselves.

Even the sensations we associate with excitement, fluttering chest, shakiness, butterflies, often get mistaken for anxiety. That's how far we've come from knowing what joy really feels like in the body.

But here's the truth: excitement is a form of truth. It shows you what matters. It reveals what you care about most. And that's why it's vulnerable. To share your excitement is to be seen, really seen, for what lights you up. No wonder it feels risky.

When this energy gets suppressed for too long, it doesn't disappear. It finds distorted outlets: drama, overreactions, compulsive distractions. These are the shadows of joy that were never allowed to breathe.

Practice: To reclaim excitement, you have to let yourself feel it again, out loud. Ask yourself:

- Where do I still suppress my excitement?
- When do I tone it down to avoid being judged?
- What would it feel like to let myself be seen in what lights me up, without

apology?

Excitement is more than a fleeting emotion. It's a compass. It points toward what gives your life energy and meaning. When you welcome it back, you reclaim a piece of your aliveness.

Craziness & Intuition: When Reality Feels Distorted

Relationships can sometimes make us feel like we're losing our minds. Our personalities can become so distorted that we rely on constant manipulation to navigate the fear of being abandoned, criticized, or humiliated. As human beings, we tend to believe what is stated, whether written in black and white or spoken by others.

However, maintaining a strong connection to our intuition, having the courage to face confrontation and disharmony, and cultivating healthy self-esteem are essential for questioning what we hear and discerning the truth. When relationships are dominated by defensive behaviors that avoid honesty and vulnerability, it's easy to feel like something is wrong, even when your partner insists otherwise. They might tell you that you're misunderstanding them, imagining things, or even blame you for the very behaviors you've pointed out in them.

This confusion creates a sense of internal conflict: should you rely on reasoning or trust your intuition? As you get caught up in endless negotiations and arguments, your gut instincts, what feels right, become overshadowed. At the same time, the cycle of argumentation feeds the feeling that you're going crazy.

Practice: The next time you find yourself in an argument, take a moment and feel what your gut tells you. Stay with the simplicity and rawness of what you sense, and give it expression. Step away from the argument and take time for things to settle.

Walking Your Own Path

There comes a point in life where you realize: no one else can walk your path for you. Not your partner, not your parents, not your closest friend. People may walk beside you for a time, offering love, wisdom, or companionship, but eventually, they must return to their own direction. That's the nature of it.

Your path is uniquely yours. It's shaped by how you see the world, the meanings you make of your experiences, and the deeper imprints you carry, many of which go beyond your personal story, touching family, history, and even soul-level patterns.

There may be moments when the aloneness of this truth feels sharp, when you wish someone could step in, understand it all, and carry it with you. But there's also something sacred in this solitude. It reminds you that your life is your own to live. Your choices, your growth, your becoming, they're not meant to be outsourced.

Walking your own path is not about isolation. It's about ownership. And when you walk it fully, you become more capable of offering true companionship to others on their journey, without needing to merge, fix, or be saved.

Chapter 2: Seeing with New Eyes

The familiar has a way of quietly settling into our minds as "known." We think we understand a theme, a dynamic, a formula, until life asks us to look again. This chapter is an invitation to revisit what you believe you already see clearly and to notice how time, experience, and growth may have shifted your perspective.

Often, we approach life's tensions by choosing sides, seeking certainty over doubt, closeness over space, freedom over responsibility. But much of living is about allowing contradictions to coexist without forcing resolution. Here, we explore how widening your perspective can soften old conclusions, revealing that the richness of life often lies not in the answers but in the space between them.

Growth Through Discomfort

What makes growth so complex, and at times painful, is that it rarely follows a straight line. Life keeps drawing us into cycles of connection and separation, requiring us to rebuild trust, reorient ourselves, and start again. We long for something solid to hold on to, a clear conclusion about who we are. Yet deep down, we sense that anything fixed or final will always feel incomplete.

True growth asks you to show up more fully, not because it's easy, but because the cost of inner division becomes too painful. It's not about forcing change but allowing parts of you to fall away through honest inclusion. Growth isn't the opposite of doubt or failure, it depends on them. These uncomfortable states are not detours; they are the terrain.

On Being Normal

When we set aside extreme cases of violence or severe psychological disorders, many of the painful experiences people carry, rejection, humiliation, emotional neglect, even forms of abuse, are quite common. Though these experiences can be heartbreaking, they're not signs of personal failure. They're part of what it means to be human.

Yet we often treat these experiences as if they're shameful exceptions, as if our pain proves we're broken or different from everyone else. We look at others and assume they've escaped what we've endured. This sense of being "the only one" intensifies suffering and isolates us from the very connection that could help us heal.

But what if these struggles weren't disqualifying? What if they were simply . . . normal? Not acceptable. Not ideal. But part of life.

To see your pain as part of the human condition doesn't mean minimizing it. It means placing it in a larger, more compassionate context, one that lets you approach your experiences with less shame and more curiosity.

One of the greatest challenges in this cultural moment is not to be exceptional, impressive, or constantly improving, but to allow yourself to be normal. To carry both wounds and resilience. To know that you are not alone in your struggle, and that being human was never meant to be perfect.

Choosing to Show Up

There's a distinct energetic difference between being given responsibility and asking to take it. The latter comes from within, it says, "I want to participate. I want to take care of something." It's a voluntary act that originates from inner will and agency.

When responsibility is assigned, you inherit a predefined framework and the expectations that come with it. Your role becomes about meeting someone else's standard, not necessarily your own. But when you ask for responsibility, you set the tone. You create the framework, challenge yourself to deliver, and show others they can count on you. This kind of self-initiated responsibility is more empowering, more intentional, and has the potential to bring you closer to understanding who you really are.

And yet, many of us hesitate to ask. We've been taught that responsibility comes with pressure, judgment, or the risk of failing in front of others. Perhaps we were given too much too soon, and so we've learned to associate responsibility with burden rather than agency.

But asking for responsibility is not about control or perfection. It's a quiet declaration of presence. It says, "I'm here. I'm willing." It's how we step into life with clarity and purpose, not to prove something, but to belong to it more fully.

The Respect We Didn't Grow Up With

Respect is often mistaken for politeness. We think it means agreeing, being nice, or staying quiet. But at its core, respect is something deeper: the willingness to listen, truly listen, with openness, presence, and curiosity.

To respect someone is to make space for who they are, even when it challenges you. It's not about approval. It's about contact.

Many of us grew up in environments where respect was conditional or absent altogether. Maybe the adults around you were overwhelmed, volatile, or emotionally unavailable. To survive, you adapted, staying small, staying quiet, reading the room instead of expressing yourself. You may have played a role: the strong one, the easy one, the peacemaker, the caretaker. These roles helped you avoid rejection but came at the cost of authenticity.

Over time, those protective roles become part of your identity. They limit choice and keep you from being seen as you truly are. Deep down, you sense the inauthenticity, expressions of superiority or inferiority don't reflect your real self. This awareness can bring frustration or pain, especially when a partner's actions trigger old wounds. But those wounds are reminders of what's seeking to be healed, and the roles are signposts pointing to where we've lost connection with ourselves.

Healing doesn't mean demanding that others prove our worth by treating us a certain way. It means reclaiming the parts of us that learned to hide. It means recognizing that our vulnerability is not a weakness but a form of honesty, and allowing it to be seen.

In relationships, respect isn't about erasing differences or avoiding conflict. It's about holding those differences without retreating, reacting, or needing to win. It's the quiet strength of saying, "I may not fully understand you, but I'm here, and I want to be."

To give and receive that kind of listening is one of the most intimate and healing acts we can offer. It's how we move from playing roles to truly meeting each other.

The Right to Take Responsibility

Responsibility isn't just a duty. At its best, it's a way of claiming your own importance in the world. But many of us grow up learning a different story: We take on responsibility out of sacrifice, guilt, or a desperate need for validation. We learn that being "good" means carrying weight for others, not because it feels right, but because we fear what will happen if we don't.

When you don't believe you deserve to matter, responsibility feels like a burden. You take it on resentfully, or you avoid it altogether, fearing that stepping up will only cost you freedom, energy, or connection.

True responsibility feels different. It's not something you inherit blindly or bear grudgingly. It's something you take, because you recognize your own relevance. Because you understand that your participation in life matters.

When responsibility is rooted in meaning instead of obligation, it nourishes you. It becomes a form of agency, not sacrifice. A way to stand fully inside your life, not shrink from it.

The shift happens when you stop asking, "What must I carry to be good?"

and start asking, "What is mine to carry because I want to be here?"

Stuckness

So many moments of hardship leave us dumbfounded, confused, or even in a state of shock. These interruptions can create a sense of stuckness, a time when it's unclear how to respond or move on. In such moments, remember that stuckness is part of the flow. Valuable lessons are hidden there. Don't resist it.

Hate Connects

Hate creates an illusion of freedom. Demonizing others provides justification for keeping your distance, avoiding closeness, and evading any sense of obligation or responsibility toward them. However, this sense of freedom is deceptive. Paradoxically, hatred limits your actual freedom by binding you obsessively to the object of your hatred, creating a connection that is anything but liberating.

Secrecy: Power, Not Just Shame

Secrecy is not just about hiding in shame, it can also be a way of preserving power, agency, and freedom. To keep something private is not always a sign of fear or guilt; it can be a deliberate act of self-containment, a refusal to expose what is not yet ready, or a protection of one's inner life from external influence.

Practicing Alignment

As we move toward greater alignment with ourselves, finding our own way, our truth, and our agency, we often pass through a stage of strong, charged assertions. In claiming power and often independence, we may say things like, "I'm done with this," "I don't care anymore," or "I don't owe you anything."

These statements can feel bold and decisive, but as long as they carry emotional charge, you haven't fully arrived. You're still practicing, trying on new positions, testing how they feel, and using them to push against what no longer fits.

Over time, practice ripens into something quieter. The words lose their edge and settle into a truth that resonates deeply, bringing both relief and vulnerability. This is the moment you're no longer reacting but standing in a position that feels more like home.

Acceptance as Transcendence

Acceptance might itself be transcendence, rather than seeking to transcend what feels unwanted.

Adulthood as an Ongoing Process of Maturation

You may associate adulthood with age, but there are moments when the child within still runs the show, even as you perform adult roles. Internally, you might feel like an impostor, weak, uncertain, or disconnected. Growing up often brings a profound sense of loss, such as losing love, recognition, respect, or care from parents or other significant figures. Instead of understanding this loss and seeking alternative mentors to fill what was missing, you may find yourself waiting for something that can no longer come.

This waiting can persist indefinitely, keeping you stuck in a childlike longing. Maturing takes you beyond this waiting. It invites you to acknowledge your inner duality, the coexistence of light and shadow, vulnerability and strength, while remaining open to support and guidance. This process is neither linear nor destination-bound; it is a continuous redefinition of yourself, informed by life and your evolving role within it.

Maturity doesn't seek to eliminate fear or pain but teaches you to stop avoiding the discomfort they bring. It reveals itself in your ability to stay present without resorting to manipulation, drama, or retreat. While the child energy within you is unpredictable and uncertain, the adult energy is grounded, clear, and intentional. Maturity doesn't mean suppressing childlike tendencies but navigating them with wisdom. It embraces life's limitations and the reality that you "can't have it all," empowering you to act from a place of embodied clarity rather than reactivity.

Practice: Table 1 illustrates the feelings and experiences associated with both the adult and the child within. This distinction provides a tangible framework, inviting you to reflect on your own experiences. The purpose of this reflection is not self-judgment but to serve as an entry point for contemplation. It is natural to identify with some, but not all, of the feelings described in the table and to experience emotions that may seem contradictory, reflecting an identification with aspects from both columns.

Once you've gone through both columns, return to the left side, the "mature adult." Choose 1-2 aspects that resonate for you, and take moments throughout your day to embody them. This way, you gradually bring an embodied memory into your reality, allowing you to show up for yourself and others in more grounded ways.

Adult, personified as maturation	*Child, active in us as adults*
• The adult has a clear internal compass, knowing what to do and what feels right (not about an absolute truth, but an inner sense of alignment).	• The child is uncertain about what to do or what is right, still seeking guidance.
• The adult embodies a clear identity that can be felt and recognized by others. They allow this identity to confine and define them.	• The child is in the process of forming an identity and is unclear how to go about it.
• The adult acknowledges his/her limitations and embraces the weight and meaning of responsibility.	• The child seeks freedom from limitation, obligation, and responsibility, often taking on risks as a means to meaning, and tasks out of fear or a need for recognition.
• The adult feels comfortable in its own skin, grounded in its sense of self.	• The child looks for external validation, constantly checking: "Who notices me? Did I do something wrong? Did I do well?". It is shy or flirtatious, unsure of its own boundaries.
• What the adult says carries weight for themselves and others; it reflects intentionality and purpose.	• What the child says feels weightless to it, lacking the sense it can have an impact.
• The adult seeks confrontation where needed and looks for resolution.	• The child is reactive, shying away from confrontation or looking for provocation, but doesn't feel nourished by the outcome from either.
• The adult understands and accepts the consequences of taking on responsibility.	• The child seeks to be unburdened from responsibility and excused if something goes wrong.

Table 1. How the adult and child express themselves through us

CHAPTER 2: SEEING WITH NEW EYES

The Limits of Integration

You often hear about psychological or emotional integration, especially after significant life events, personal realizations, or transformative experiences. Perhaps you've gone through a painful separation, uncovered a hidden personality trait, or returned from a transformational workshop. Integration begins with understanding, grasping the new ideas, frameworks, or truths you've been presented with.

For instance, if you lose a loved one, the initial wave of grief might overwhelm you, but soon you encounter the unfolding process of mourning, a cycle that often begins with denial. Understanding these stages gives you a framework to navigate your emotions, but true integration goes beyond the conceptual. It requires practice and embodiment, where these insights and truths become lived experiences rather than mere intellectual knowledge.

Yet, even after this embodiment, a layer of inner duality and complexity often remains. Integration is not about erasing this duality but accepting it. It is about reconciling the tensions within you and holding space for the contradictions that make you human. This deeper integration transcends concepts.

The Trap of Idealism

Idealism can feel like a kind of elevation. It can make you feel special, separate, even superior, aligned with a cause, a vision, a hope bigger than yourself. In idealism, it's easy to believe you are standing for what is noble and good.

But over time, idealism can pull you away from something more personal: your own story. Instead of being rooted in your individuality and lived experience, you become more attached to the idea you represent. You start to lose touch with yourself, not only in how others see you, but in how you perceive yourself.

Idealism often grows from unhealed hurt. It gives structure to earlier experiences of humiliation, betrayal, or powerlessness. When life felt unfair or painful, idealism offered a larger narrative where you could be right, protected, and good.

This isn't wrong, it's a human way of coping. But if you live too long inside the ideal without revisiting the original hurt, the ideal hardens. It becomes righteousness. It turns into a subtle form of aggression, defending the idea even at the cost of real connection with others or with yourself.

If you look carefully, you may find that behind your strongest ideals lies a softer, more vulnerable truth: a grief you didn't know how to name, a longing for fairness, a hope that life could be kinder or that your concerns could be taken seriously.

Practice: Think of one ideal you represent or hold strongly, about the world, a cause, yourself. Then ask yourself:

- Which part of the ideal matters to me?
- What early experience of hurt, disappointment, or hope do I relate to the ideal?

Notice if allowing yourself to feel the human story behind the ideal helps soften the way you hold it.

When Belonging Replaces Integrity

Living in an open society gives us the opportunity to express our truths, share our vulnerabilities, and find solidarity. But when personal truth hardens into absolute truth, something essential gets lost. The more we seek belonging through shared ideology, the more pressure we feel to align perfectly with the group, to say the right things, hold the right beliefs, and avoid making mistakes.

At first, this can feel safe. It offers a sense of certainty and connection. But over time, it creates a deeper insecurity: the fear of being wrong, the fear of being cast out. Movements that once aimed to heal, whether political, cultural, or spiritual, can start to mirror the very exclusion they hoped to end.

Conformity replaces curiosity. Righteousness replaces dialogue.

One of the hidden forces behind this rigidity is collective guilt. When guilt becomes widespread, people often focus more on relieving it, proving their goodness, than on making choices that feel true to them. Self-expression becomes less about honesty and more about performance. Vulnerability becomes strategic. Truth becomes distorted by the need to belong.

Instead of using guilt as a doorway into deeper self-reflection, many take it up as a shield, hiding behind ideology, avoiding the more difficult work of facing their own complexity and contradictions.

The cost is high. When we give up our individuality for the safety of the group, we lose the very thing that makes connection real: our willingness to stay rooted in ourselves even when it's uncomfortable.

True belonging doesn't demand perfect alignment. It asks for integrity, the courage to show up whole, not flawless.

Harmony

True harmony requires resilience to conflict. Without the ability to navigate disagreements and tensions, harmony becomes superficial, fragile and easily disrupted by the challenges of real connection. Genuine harmony is built not in the absence of conflict but through the willingness to face it with openness and mutual respect.

On Truth in Relationships

Truth is hard to handle, it has no compassion or kindness; it simply is. Our love seeks to be romantic, but truth cannot be. Yet, even truth isn't absolute. In relationships, some space for untruth or occasional pretense is necessary to prevent excessive strain. This is a core challenge of authentic relating.

The Simplicity of Hardship

When you are feeling good, you are good; when you are feeling bad, it feels bad. The fortunate among us remember that we shift between these states many times throughout life. This awareness helps you hold the "bad" times with greater perspective, reminding you of their impermanence and allowing you to move through them with less overwhelm.

It's simple: life is hard. Accepting this makes it easier to face and say yes to the challenges we meet.

Wisdom

Wisdom often comes with age because, over time, you encounter countless opportunities to try and fail, to try and succeed, to manipulate, to betray, and to face the consequences of those actions. It is not something that can be easily transferred through words. It is rooted in personal experience, shaped by the scars and humility gained through living. Wisdom carries the weight of personal trials and the understanding that no lesson comes without a price.

Stop Trying to Change, That's When It Happens

We often seek change because we're uncomfortable with who we are. But when change is driven by a need to escape, rather than a sense of inner alignment, it becomes forced, and often doesn't last. Real transformation, ironically, tends to happen when we stop trying so hard to change and start becoming curious about who we already are.

For example, if you decide to become a vegetarian, you may feel the need to justify it with a specific belief system. If you later choose to stop being vegetarian, you might again rationalize the shift. Rarely do we allow ourselves to say, "It was there, and now it has passed." Instead, change is often burdened by justifications, measured by how acceptable it is to those around us. True change happens when the protections you once relied upon are no longer necessary. If, for example, you develop greater self-esteem, you may no longer feel the need to keep secrets. This change does not stem from an external justification but from an inner shift that allows you to speak about your experiences with ease, without needing to control how you are perceived.

We don't change easily because our personalities are deeply shaped by the need for safety, they're complex systems built to protect us. But over time, certain patterns, needs, fears, and worries can begin to fall away on their own. Each time that happens, you move a little closer to feeling at home within yourself. Interestingly, the more you chase change, the more you may be operating from an ego-driven place that resists parts of who you truly are.

Instead of forcing change, genuine transformation happens when you cultivate curiosity about who you have become. This openness weakens defenses, allowing what was once repressed to surface naturally. Knowing and accepting yourself leads to a lightness, an ability to not take yourself too seriously. With this acceptance, aspects of your personality structure can soften and even dissolve.

Victimhood and Responsibility

The term "victim" is often used in conversations, with phrases like, "You're acting like a victim" or "Don't be such a victim." But what does it truly mean to embody a victim-like mentality or to remain stuck in the experience of victimhood? At its core, victimhood involves a seemingly passive engagement with life, where your own aggression, power games, agency, and will appear absent. Yet beneath the surface, there is often an undercurrent of rage, righteousness, and even a sense of superiority.

When you slip into a victim mentality, something within you waits, waiting for attention or resolution of your issues through the actions of others. Yet, paradoxically, you may resist resolution even when it is within reach. You become caught in a loop of suffering, narrating your pain without seeking progress. The essence of victimhood lies in avoiding forward movement and the responsibility that comes with it. Responsibility in this context might mean letting go of demands for protection and stepping into the vulnerability of trial and error, of succeeding and failing.

To step out of this cycle, you must confront the hidden power dynamics beneath your victimhood. This involves recognizing the ways you use aggression and manipulation to maintain your narrative of justified suffering, instead of embracing the discomfort and limitations of freedom that come with responsibility. Breaking free from victimhood demands the courage to let go of the protective shield you've built around your pain. It requires a willingness to accept support and guidance as pathways to reclaiming your strength, agency, and ability to engage with life on more authentic terms.

Hope Isn't Naive, It's Necessary

Hope is often misunderstood. Some see it as naive, too soft, too light, too wishful to carry any real weight. But if you've ever come through heartbreak, illness, failure, or grief… then you know: hope is not a decoration. It's fuel.

Hope is what keeps you upright when everything else says to fall. It's what lets you take the next step when the outcome is still unknown. It doesn't promise clarity, it whispers possibility.

Think of hope like a battery. It charges and drains depending on what you go through, what you believe, and how the world meets you. Some days it runs low. But even the smallest spark, an image, a song, a stranger's kindness, can recharge it just enough to move you forward again.

And inspiration? That's just hope in motion. It's the reminder that something beautiful, meaningful, or healing is still possible, even if you can't see it yet.

Hope isn't a luxury. It's how we survive. And more than that, it's how we grow.

The Fear and Relief of Being Seen

Deep down, we long to be seen for who we really are, beyond the roles we play or the image we project. We desire someone to look at us and recognize something true, something real. And yet, being seen is also terrifying.

Because beneath our practiced smiles and polished explanations, many of us fear that what's underneath isn't enough. We worry that if someone looks too closely, they'll find the imposter, the part of us that still feels unworthy, unfinished, or flawed.

Much of what we do to survive, our strategies, our performances, our subtle acts of self-protection, is aimed at controlling how others perceive us. We try to manage the risk of exposure, to stay safe from rejection, judgment, or disappointment.

But connection doesn't come from controlling how we're seen. It comes from allowing ourselves to be seen as we are, imperfect, human, real. Being seen is never just comfortable. But it is, perhaps, one of the most healing experiences we can have.

Practice: Notice today where you hold back a piece of yourself, where you smile, nod, or stay quiet to avoid being fully seen. You don't have to change it right away. Just notice it. Awareness is the first step toward allowing more of yourself to come forward, without apology.

The Journey to Trustworthiness

Being seen and regarded as trustworthy is often something we expect from those around us. Yet, trustworthiness is not something we inherently possess, it must be cultivated. Your personality, shaped as a strategy for belonging and recognition, is fundamentally an adaptation. While this adaptation helps you navigate the world and stay safe, it often prevents you from being fully trustworthy because it prioritizes protection over authenticity.

As we mature, we begin to understand the limitations imposed by past hurts, values, culture, and conditioning. We are not blank slates. The clearer and more defined you become, by making your values and boundaries conscious, the more trustworthy you can be. Trustworthiness requires integration: a person who deeply understands their protective mechanisms and can openly and vulnerably acknowledge them is better positioned to be trusted.

That said, trustworthiness is often partial or situational. Even as we work to integrate and grow, we may still have blind spots or areas where we struggle. Accepting this incongruence within yourself, acknowledging that you are not automatically trustworthy, requires great humility. Yet, the process of becoming trustworthy in your own eyes may be one of the most fulfilling journeys you can undertake in life.

The Grip of Fear

When fear colors our experiences of life, it becomes more difficult to truly know ourselves and grow in awareness. Fear acts as a veil, filtering our perceptions and shaping our expectations with constant anticipation of negative outcomes, such as rejection or humiliation. It seeks to simplify the complexity of life, which it perceives as dangerous and confusing, reducing it to binary terms of good or bad.

The more fear dominates us, the more the outside world feels hostile and in need of defense. We stop seeing reality for what it is and instead project our fears onto it. This distortion creates a cycle: fear fuels a sense of vulnerability, which then transforms into aggression disguised as self-protection. We may remain unaware of the attacks we launch in the name of defense, consumed by the drive to shield ourselves.

But fear also manifests in deeply personal ways. If you cannot face, contain, and be truthful about your own fears, you risk remaining disconnected from reality and unable to perceive the richness and nuance of life. Awareness requires moving beyond fear's flattening grasp and embracing the complexities of life with courage and openness.

The Illusion of Being Special

It's more meaningful to view ourselves as unique, allowing something within us to express itself differently from others, rather than perpetuating the illusion that we are special. When we aim to be special, we set ourselves apart in a way that demands being "more than" others.

Have you ever felt trapped in maintaining an image of being special? The pursuit of specialness can lead to a self-created prison, where you feel compelled to sustain that identity. Consumed by the need to be different, you may reject the wisdom, knowledge, and creativity that already exist.

This attachment to being special limits your ability to explore other aspects of who you are. The harder you strive to be special, the more you constrain your capacity to discover what truly matters to you and to forge your own authentic path.

Part II - Reflections on Family and Intimate Relationships

Introduction

Across family life, friendships, and intimate partnerships, our patterns are influenced by both personal history and collective inheritance. The wish to be liked, the pull of suffering as a way to connect, the confusion around needs and boundaries, the difficulty of choosing, and the complexity of attachment are not isolated problems. They all point to the same essential movement: a search for balance between self and other, freedom and belonging, strength and humility. The ideal of love may never be fully reached, but the work of learning to love remains central. Each relationship, however imperfect, invites us to see what still needs to be met, healed, or reclaimed within ourselves.

Relationships shape us from the beginning. Family is our first and most enduring imprint. The lives, values, and unhealed wounds of those who came before us continue within us, influencing how we love, protect, and how we care for those in our lives. Healing family bonds is not about rewriting the past, but about seeing more clearly who our parents and grandparents were, grieving what could not be given, and honoring what was. From this clarity, we reclaim the freedom to live by our own values and to parent with intention. Roots and guidance, values and boundaries, the quiet hope we hold for our children, and the ability to trust their journey all become part of how we shape the next generation.

Beyond the family, relationships are woven from small, daily exchanges. How we give and receive, speak truth, set limits, show up, withdraw, and repair becomes the fabric of connection. Many of our struggles here are subtle. We may give without receiving, or receive without giving. We may confuse empathy with overextension, mistake drama for depth, or protect ourselves with isolation, approval seeking, or unfinished business. This chapter looks at these threads between us and at the practices that move us from reaction to action, from waiting to be chosen to stepping forward, from vague headlines to honest, precise expression.

Intimate relationships bring these themes into a sharper and often more vulnerable focus. The couple carries both a shared journey and two individual ones, shaped by attachment, desire, and the tension between safety and growth. The same longing that draws us close can also make us afraid to show who we are becoming. We may cling to roles or fantasies, avoid compromise, or fear that honesty will cost us belonging. Yet real intimacy asks us to hold security and change together, to let more than one truth exist in the same space, and to accept that love alone is rarely enough without clarity, effort, and mutual responsibility.

While it may be wise not to take the ideal of love too seriously, the lesson of love and the journey of learning to love remain vital. We're always in the right relationship, no matter how wrong or painful it may seem. "Right" doesn't mean good, but rather fitting, aligned with the blind spots we carry and the self-esteem we still need to cultivate. Separation or divorce is often the attempt to find better alignment between your values and actions, as well as reclaiming a sense of self-esteem.

Relationships invite us, again and again, to experience and rediscover what love is, to understand who we are through the other, and to be seen in our confusing duality. They require us to embrace balance, which demands humility, as well as living with our limitations. To truly grasp the full meaning of relationships, we must reframe and expand our perspectives, moving beyond often one-dimensional beliefs about love and connection.

Chapter 3: Healing Family Bonds

Family shapes us in ways both visible and unseen. The lives, struggles, values, and unhealed wounds of those who came before us live on in us, influencing how we love, protect, and define ourselves. Healing family bonds is not about rewriting the past but about seeing it clearly, recognizing our parents as imperfect people, grieving what could not be given, and honoring what was. In doing so, we reclaim the freedom to parent with intention, live by our own values, and trust the journeys of those who come after us.

Understanding Yourself Through Your Past

To know yourself, you must take a sincere interest in who your parents and grandparents were and the challenges they faced to survive. Embodying their lives and struggles expands your capacity to understand what you're made of, rather than clinging to the illusion that you can simply "be yourself" in isolation.

You inherit both your DNA and your past, forces that can feel limiting, yet also provide a starting point. While you're never entirely free from them, honoring where you come from is what makes it possible to move forward with integrity into your own future.

Recognizing the Person Behind the Parent

Healing your relationship with your parents begins when you can look at the past more realistically, and see your parents not just as "parents," but as people. Behind the mother or father you longed for stand two individuals shaped by their own upbringing, struggles, and unresolved wounds.

Most parents are not equipped to live up to the mythical expectations we place upon them. They pass down not only love and guidance but also the unresolved burdens and survival strategies inherited from generations before them. When you cling to the fantasy that they could have been different, you trap yourself in cycles of blame, anger, and unmet longing.

Letting go of the myth is painful. It confronts a deep and tender part of you, the part that longs to feel completely safe, loved, and accepted without reservation. Recognizing that this absolute safety may never have fully existed can stir grief and even resistance. Yet facing this truth allows you to move beyond illusion into something more genuine.

Real healing begins when you stop holding your parents hostage to idealized roles they could never fully inhabit. It requires accepting what was given, no matter how imperfectly, and grieving what could not be given.

This shift demands both humility and grief: humility to see your parents' limits without moral superiority, and grief for the love, safety, or recognition that may have been missing. It allows you to meet them, and yourself, with greater honesty, compassion, and maturity.

By seeing your parents as the imperfect people they are, you free yourself. You step out of the endless waiting for something different and step into the life that is yours to live.

Roots and Guidance: The Freedom that Comes from Clarity

The less defined your own values are as a parent, the more freedom you may unintentionally give your child. In the absence of knowing what is right or important, it becomes easier to step back and let your child decide. This can look like open-mindedness, but often it reflects a discomfort with setting direction.

When you're clear about what matters to you, kindness, discipline, respect, or resilience, you can offer real guidance. Your clarity becomes a compass for your child, helping them navigate choices with greater confidence.

To imprint a child is not to restrict them, it is to give them roots. Today, many parents shy away from this, believing that too much direction limits freedom. Yet in the absence of a strong imprint, other, often harsher identities will take its place.

Roots give a child something to hold onto when life becomes uncertain. They offer belonging and orientation, a sense that there is something to return to when the world feels unstable. Freedom without belonging is fragile. We all need something to believe in, to feel part of, and to give our freedom direction.

Children don't just need freedom, they need orientation. When you lead with grounded values, you give your child both. From there, they can later choose their own way, not out of confusion, but out of connection.

Educating Our Children: A Mirror of Ourselves

Besides loving our children, perhaps the greatest responsibility we carry as parents is to transmit values, socialize them, and nurture a healthy sense of self-esteem. But while these goals are important, few of us are consciously equipped with a roadmap. In practice, much of our parenting happens intuitively, shaped by habit, emotion, and our own upbringing. We often enforce rules and boundaries without a clear understanding of how they shape our children or what objectives we want to achieve.

Because of this, we often influence our children in ways we don't fully realize. Even without deliberate intention, we help shape a personality, one that may carry internal contradictions, as many of the lessons we impart reflect our own unresolved needs more than the unique needs of our child.

A useful indicator of whether you are consciously teaching your children something is the weight and limitations you place on yourself in the process.

For instance, if you want your children to learn discipline, you must embody patience and perseverance by sitting with them and guiding them, even when it restricts your own freedom. True teaching, then, requires intentionality and self-discipline on your part, in the hope that the values you model will take root in their lives.

This kind of parenting asks more from you than reacting in the moment, it calls for alignment between what you value and how you live. And while that effort can feel exhausting or inconvenient, it's also where real influence happens: not through control, but by embodiment and knowing it's true for you.

Values Versus Boundaries: The Foundation of Meaningful Guidance

As a parent, one of your primary responsibilities is to guide and teach your children, often through setting boundaries. However, boundaries are frequently enforced as a form of aggression rather than as a healthy educational tool. In moments of frustration or anger, you may impose boundaries not out of love or a desire to teach, but as a reaction to your own unmet needs or unresolved wounds. These wounds, such as a need for respect, fear of humiliation, or the overwhelm of parenthood, often surface in interactions with your children.

As a result, what you call boundaries may be more about your own emotional struggles than about teaching or guiding your child. When enforced aggressively, boundaries fail to educate. Instead, they leave children feeling rejected, shamed, or humiliated and rarely convey the lessons you hope to instill.

This is where the distinction between boundaries and values becomes crucial. Boundaries imposed through aggression are often punitive, reactive, and tied to a need for control. In contrast, values reflect deeper truths you have integrated through lived experience. Values provide a framework for meaningful guidance, grounded in care and purpose rather than in reactionary behavior.

For example, discipline as a value is taught patiently over time because you firmly believe it benefits your child. Discipline as a boundary, however, often becomes a form of punishment, devoid of purpose or meaning. Values require thoughtful reflection and commitment; they obligate you and limit your freedom, but in doing so, they create stability and security for both you and your child.

By anchoring your parenting in values rather than boundaries, you provide a foundation for your child to grow and learn while also offering them a sense of trust and resilience as they navigate life's challenges.

Hope for Our Children: Trusting Their Journey

Our children face countless challenges as they grow. They must learn how to make friends, and how to choose the right ones. They'll navigate academic pressures, develop new skills, and grapple with the desire to live up to their potential. As parents, we hope they'll stay close to family while still discovering their own paths. Along the way, they'll face the turbulence of puberty, the lure of risk and adventure, and the weight of peer pressure, as well as the need to fit in.

In all of this, you want them to be strong, uphold values, and develop sound self-esteem. Yet, inevitably, they will stumble and fail in these endeavors, needing both reassurance and, at times, tough guidance from their parents.

This is where parenting becomes its most emotionally demanding: you're asked to stay steady while letting go, to guide without controlling, and to love without guarantees. You do your best, all while carrying the quiet fear that they may struggle in ways you can't prevent.

As a parent, you often cannot be certain they'll "make it"—whatever that means. Thus, much of parenting is about learning to live in that uncertainty with grace.

Practice: One of the greatest gifts you can give your children is to quietly hold trust in your heart and express it aloud: "You'll be okay" or "You'll make it." Even when you feel doubt, this trust is what they need most.

The Importance We Hold as Parents

As a parent, you may know in theory that you're important to your child, but you don't always feel it. In response, you might try to prove your worth by doing more, staying busy, or earning their affection. But this often misses the deeper truth: you matter to your child simply because you're their parent. Your importance isn't something you have to earn, it's already there.

Embodying this truth can profoundly shift how you experience the task of parenting. When you fail to recognize your intrinsic value to your children, you remain stuck in a cycle of trying to earn your importance through actions rather than simply feeling it.

Practice: Being able to say and genuinely believe the words *I'm important to you* is empowering for parents and deeply reassuring for children. It fosters a sense of connection and ease that benefits both sides of the relationship.

Chapter 4: The Threads Between Us

Relationships are woven from small, daily exchanges, how we give and receive, set boundaries, speak truth, tolerate difference, repair hurt, and choose each other again. These threads can be strong or fragile. When we lean too much on habit, protect ourselves with drama, or avoid closure, the fabric thins. When we risk clarity, honor limits with kindness, and allow more than one truth to exist, connection becomes steadier and more human.

This section gathers brief reflections on the practices that keep the weave alive: skillfulness over impulse, effort over entitlement, honesty without manipulation, empathy without overextension, and needs named without shame. You'll be invited to notice where you isolate, where you wait to be chosen, where absolutes replace specifics, and where disappointment asks for cleaner expectations. The aim isn't perfection, it's movement: from reaction to action, from projection to presence, from guarding the bond to tending it.

The Reciprocity of Giving and Receiving

We only begin to cultivate humility, trust, and a sense of being cared for when we allow an equal exchange of giving and receiving. In the imbalance of giving without receiving, we may feel righteous, even superior. Giving can make us feel needed and relevant, but it also disconnects us from our vulnerability and the deeper human need to belong. Ask yourself: "When you focus solely on giving, do you find yourself avoiding asking for what you truly need? Is your generosity *quietly* hoping for something in return?"

Similarly, those who prefer receiving without giving back often seek to shield themselves from the obligations and responsibilities that come with close connections. It's a false innocence that seeks to be preserved.

This imbalance, whether in giving or receiving, keeps relationships guarded and inauthentic. Allowing a balanced flow of giving and receiving nurtures trust and mutual vulnerability, the foundation of meaningful relationships.

Cultivating Skillfulness in Relationships

Our personalities, full of patterns, wounds, and defenses, often introduce conflict that threatens the sacred bond of a relationship. We want to become skillful in protecting the bond and promise we share.

Accepting that something precious needs protection makes us vulnerable. It forces us to acknowledge that relationships are fragile and can be lost, sometimes easily. In moments of anger, vengefulness, or righteousness, it can even feel momentarily satisfying to lash out, to hurt, or to withdraw, as destruction demands less effort than preservation.

But to nurture and sustain what we have built requires cultivating skillfulness. Skillfulness is not perfection. It is made of sensitivity, the ability to notice what is happening beyond words; logic, to understand when emotion clouds judgment; patience, to endure when things feel messy or unresolved; and humility, to accept our own role in conflict.

When we attune to these qualities, we move from reacting impulsively to navigating relationships with deeper care and intention. Skillfulness transforms love from a fragile accident into a conscious act of devotion.

Connection Requires Effort

Connection is about genuine contact, but it doesn't arise just because a relationship exists. True connection requires intentionality, openness, and a willingness to show up, even when it's uncomfortable. Letting go of the belief that connection should be effortless is essential; it's something cultivated through presence, vulnerability, and shared investment.

Here lies the paradox: while authentic connection often feels natural and unforced, it usually takes real effort to get there. When you first "click" with someone, you feel connected effortlessly, but that's most likely because the connection is fueled by projection rather than reality. Once some of those projections are rolled back and "the other" becomes visible, we must move through our defenses, discomfort, and old patterns to reach that space of connection.

The effort may feel unnatural or like resistance at first, but it's precisely in choosing to engage, despite fear, ideal, or habit, that we create room for connection to unfold. It's not the absence of effort that makes connection real, but the kind of effort that comes from the heart and seeks to end separation.

The Weight of Unfinished Business

Without closure, parts of our lives remain suspended, paused in a kind of emotional holding pattern. This sense of incompletion may seem small at first, but over time, it creates an invisible weight that subtly shapes how we show up in the present.

Social rituals like saying "thank you" or offering a genuine "goodbye" give us micro-closures that help maintain emotional clarity. But when something matters deeply, especially in relationships, we often avoid closure. Not just out of anger or pride, but because closure confirms finality. It asks us to grieve, to let go of hope, or to face what we wished had turned out differently.

Avoiding endings can keep us tethered to old identities, roles, or fantasies. We may stay stuck in relationships long after they've ended, mentally rehearsing conversations, holding on to resentment, or silently waiting for acknowledgment that may never come. This kind of open loop not only creates emotional noise but also blocks the inner space needed for renewal.

Conscious completion, whether through a conversation, a ritual, or an internal shift, supports maturity. It says, for example: "This mattered, and now it's over." Only with that acknowledgment can something new begin.

Practice: Notice areas of your life where closure is missing, unfinished conversations, vague endings, lingering hopes. Ask yourself: what would honoring this ending look like? Whether it's writing a letter, speaking your truth, or simply allowing yourself to grieve, let it end, so something else can begin.

Punishing Isolation

Self-imposed isolation is often a way of punishing those around you for the guilt and unworthiness you feel within yourself. By withdrawing, you project your inner struggle outward, creating distance not only from others. This act of pulling away can trap you in a cycle of disconnection, reinforcing the very feelings of guilt and inadequacy you're trying to escape.

But beneath the urge to isolate is often a quiet longing, to be seen, to be understood without having to perform or pretend. The path out of isolation doesn't start with others reaching in, but with your own willingness to reach out, even in small ways. Choosing connection, despite fear, despite shame, is what begins to restore trust in yourself and in others.

Boundaries Are Fluid

Holding boundaries is a lifelong practice. They're tested, misunderstood, or crossed, and in response, we try to assert ourselves by setting limits. But boundaries aren't like national borders, clearly mapped and respected. They exist in the tension between expressing who we are and staying connected to others.

We often hear that good boundaries require clarity. And they do. But they also require kindness, both for others and for ourselves. Clarity without care can feel sharp or cold. Kindness without clarity can feel confusing or even self-erasing. We need both, but holding them together is rarely easy.

Take, for example, the moment you need to tell a friend you can't meet their expectations. Saying "I can't" might be honest, but without warmth, it can land as rejection. On the other hand, softening your 'no' too much might leave your message unclear. The real challenge lies in staying connected to truth without abandoning care.

Boundary conversations are often framed too simply: as acts of self-assertion. But they're more than that. They are emotional negotiations, between kindness and clarity, connection and autonomy, truth and tenderness. Boundaries don't have to be rigid to be real. When held with intention, they can protect your wholeness and preserve the relationship.

Honesty or Hidden Manipulation?

Often, the impulse to say "Let me tell you what I think" arises when something has triggered you. It feels urgent, necessary, as if speaking your truth will restore balance or make things right.

But truth, when used carelessly, can quickly become something else. It can become a way to control, manipulate, or engage in subtle power struggles. You may find yourself using "my truth" aggressively to demand change, or framing "my vulnerability" in a way that quietly pressures others to act or feel a certain way.

When truth is weaponized through anger, blame, or victimhood, it loses its sincerity. Instead of being an opening for connection, it becomes a strategy to influence or steer outcomes. And while it may offer temporary relief or a sense of control, it ultimately cuts off deeper possibilities for understanding and growth.

Real honesty is not about forcing others to see your truth. It's about being willing to reveal yourself, to express what you are experiencing, without controlling how it will be received. This kind of honesty is vulnerable. It acknowledges that speaking your truth is only the beginning of a larger conversation, not the final word. It invites exploration rather than shutting it down.

Whenever you feel the impulse to "tell someone your truth," it can be powerful to pause and ask yourself:

- Am I speaking to connect, or to control?
- Am I revealing myself, or trying to manage the outcome?

Honesty leaves space for both your truth and the truth of the other. It doesn't seek to win. It seeks to understand.

Making Room for More Than One Truth

The words you choose shape not just your conversations, but your entire way of relating to life. One small but powerful example is the word but. Often, it acts like a wall. It divides ideas, shuts down curiosity, and signals contradiction. It says: Either this, or that, but not both.

- *"I love you, but I'm angry."*
- *"I want to rest, but I have work."*
- *"This feels right, but I'm afraid."*

Each time you use but, you risk dismissing the part that came before it, both in your own experience and in your connection with others.
Practice: Try using 'and' instead.

- *"I love you, and I'm angry."*
- *"I want to rest, and I have work."*
- *"This feels right, and I'm afraid."*

This small shift invites more openness, more honesty, and more emotional complexity. It allows seemingly opposite truths to coexist, just as they do in real life. It makes space for contradictions, and in doing so, brings you closer to your own wholeness and to deeper connection with others.

The Need to Know Yourself

Another can only have you, and you can only give yourself, to the extent that you have yourself. If you are scattered, unexamined, or estranged from your inner world, then what you offer is fragmented. Presence, intimacy, and meaningful giving require inner coherence. Self-possession isn't about control; it's about rootedness. It means knowing where you stand, what you feel, and what you value so that when you show up in a relationship, it's not out of compulsion, need, or performance, but from a center that's your own.

The Role of Compromise

Avoiding compromise often signals an internal resistance to life itself. It can reveal how much you "take" from life without fully engaging in its natural give-and-take. Many people resist compromise out of a fear of losing freedom, yet this fear often stems from a deeper disconnection, from the idea that accepting limits means losing a sense of being unique or special.

Compromise is essential because life inherently involves limitations. Every meaningful choice, whether in relationships, work, parenting, or friendships, demands trade-offs. While you may equate "flow" with ease, life is rarely easy. Compromise doesn't mean surrendering; it allows you to engage with life's natural rhythms, building resilience and deepening connection.

Conversely, resisting compromise reinforces the illusion of self-sufficiency, leaving you isolated and disconnected from the interdependence that defines human existence. Accepting compromise as part of life allows for greater flexibility, connection, and a deeper alignment with what truly matters.

Presence

When you're present, you don't merge or become identified with what you encounter. Presence fosters connection without attachment; it allows for the experience of contact while maintaining the integrity of your own sense of self.

The Challenge of Authenticity

Authenticity is something many of us desire, yet it remains deeply challenging to embody. The confusion often lies in the question: What is authentic and what isn't? Human nature is marked by constant inner movement and change, which can make it difficult to form a consistent image of ourselves, both to the outside world and within. In the pursuit of belonging, you may suppress what you know deep down, favoring approval over integrity.

Authenticity means standing in both our light and our darkness, requiring a deep commitment to truth. It involves showing up as who you are in a given moment, rather than clinging to ideals or trying to appear flawless. It asks you to take responsibility for your inconsistencies and be honest about them instead of using morality or idealism as a shield to protect yourself from discomfort.

Authenticity is not about seeking acceptance, forgiveness, or validation from others. It's about embracing the complexity, confusion, and contradictions within you. By loving the truth of who you are, however messy or inconsistent, it becomes possible to live authentically, not as a fixed state, but as a dynamic and evolving expression of yourself.

The Difference Between Reaction and Action

When we react, we are usually countering or opposing something that has come our way. The impulse is outward-focused, meant to provoke a response, shape how we are seen, or influence what another person feels. In this way, reaction often carries tension, even when it's subtle.

Action, by contrast, originates from within. It comes from alignment, a quiet knowing that feels true in your body, bringing a sense of ease rather than urgency. It's not aimed at proving a point or retaliating; it's a movement that affirms what matters to you, whether or not anyone else understands.

Where reaction seeks a mirror in others, action stands on its own. It solidifies your position without turning it into a weapon, allowing you to move from truth rather than from the echo of someone else's impact.

The Complexity of Attachment

Attachment is one of life's most complex themes. On the one hand, it gives you a sense of connection, identity, and purpose. The depth of love you feel for others, so powerful it makes you fear losing them, is only possible because of attachment. Without it, you might find a kind of freedom, but that freedom can feel rootless. You lose the sense of home and belonging that makes life meaningful.

Yet the stronger your attachments, the more they can limit you. Deep loyalty, to people, identities, or ideas, can keep you from exploring new parts of yourself or embracing different perspectives. It can dull your intuition and slow your growth. Paradoxically, even the desire for freedom can become its own attachment, an idea you cling to as tightly as any relationship.

In the end, attachment isn't just a source of limitation. It's also the very ground from which meaning, love, and inner growth emerge. The task isn't to rid yourself of attachment, but to hold it consciously. It's possible to love without losing yourself, and to stay open to life even as you commit to what matters to you.

Freedom Through Truthfulness

Freedom is not the absence of pain, it is the ability to stand in what is true for you. Truthfulness carries a price: it can be rejected, misunderstood, or met with distance. At times, speaking your truth may even lead to loneliness. Yet the cost of hiding it is far greater. When you honor your truth, you choose a freedom rooted in self-respect, even if it requires you to walk alone for a while.

The Search for Balance

You naturally strive for balance and are acutely sensitive to imbalance, often attempting to correct it. This dynamic is evident in how you respond to others: when faced with arrogance, something in you instinctively wants to bring them down to earth; when confronted with pessimism, you may feel the urge to lift their spirits.

For example, in conversations with a boastful friend, you might downplay their successes to ground the interaction, while with a disheartened colleague, you might offer words of encouragement to restore their hope. These moments reflect your drive for a state of "in between"—not confined to one extreme or the other, but embracing "this and that."

However, accepting this balanced state within yourself is often more challenging. While you may strive to restore harmony in others, you often resist or deny the same equilibrium within your own life, clinging to extremes of self-doubt or overconfidence. The very sensitivity that drives you to promote balance in others can reveal where you struggle with imbalance within yourself. By noticing how you instinctively seek equilibrium in your interactions, you can begin to cultivate greater acceptance and compassion for your own complexities and contradictions.

The Pull of Drama

When you express your feelings through drama or heightened emotionality, it often reveals less about what you genuinely value and more about what you are trying to protect or project. The dramatic part of you seeks attention, amplifying the importance of your feelings and beliefs, you want to ensure you are heard. In these moments, you lose openness and curiosity, obscuring your true concerns not only from others but also from yourself.

In such states, you may lean on narratives of suffering, victimization, helplessness, or morality to substantiate your arguments, masking personal vulnerability in the process. This dynamic plays out in personal relationships and social media interactions, where outrage frequently eclipses meaningful dialogue. By dramatizing, you create distance from a deeper understanding of your helplessness and what lies at its core.

But when you soften the performance and allow yourself to feel what's beneath the need to be heard, something more genuine emerges. Vulnerability replaces spectacle. From this place, you can begin to express not just what you want others to see, but what you truly feel, and that's where connection becomes possible.

Connection Through Suffering

Shared suffering or hardships form the foundation of many friendships and relationships. It's often easier to connect when vulnerability is mutual and familiar, when someone else has felt what you've felt. This can foster deep empathy and understanding.

However, when connection is built primarily around shared suffering, it often comes with a silent contract: "I will hold your pain if you hold mine." While this can feel supportive, it may create an unspoken expectation to avoid challenging one another. In this dynamic, offering honest feedback or expressing personal growth that moves beyond the shared pain can feel like a betrayal of the bond. Over time, this can limit meaningful reflection and reinforce stuckness, ultimately preventing a more authentic and evolving connection.

For example, friends may connect over the difficulty of being single and the challenges of searching for a partner. Yet, when one person moves on and finds a relationship, the bond through shared hardship often weakens, and the once-powerful connection fades. This dynamic frequently plays out in ideological, personal, and professional contexts, where solidarity through struggle becomes the primary glue of the relationship.

In contrast, connecting through strength is more challenging. Our survival and competitive instincts often create barriers to openness and collaboration. Moreover, we are often uncomfortable with strength in ourselves and others, focusing on loopholes, inconsistencies, and flaws.

Consider how you connect with others. Do you feel more at ease bonding over shared struggles than shared strengths? What motivates the way you relate to people? Becoming aware of these patterns can offer valuable insights. It allows you to identify your comfort zones around strengths and weaknesses, confront areas of difficulty or shame in expressing strength, and recognize the ways you exert control or seek attention in relationships.

By reflecting on these dynamics, you can move beyond connections rooted solely in hardship and begin fostering bonds that honor both strength and vulnerability, creating a more balanced and authentic foundation for relationships.

The Trap of Approval: Choosing Truth Over Being Liked

When the desire to be liked takes precedence, self-expression becomes filtered, and choices are shaped more by external validation than by inner conviction. The pursuit of approval distorts creativity, leading to safe, predictable actions rather than your unique voice. Over time, this need for acceptance erodes self-trust and limits the risks necessary for growth and fulfillment. True potential begins to unfold when approval becomes secondary to authenticity, when choices stem from integrity rather than fear of rejection. That's when your life starts to feel like your own.

Practice: Next time you find yourself choosing approval over your gut feeling, pause. Scan your body for any tightness, rigidity, or hesitation. Take a deep breath, close your eyes, and imagine embracing what you want to do or express. Feel the inner movement, the pull toward your own will. Sense the integrity that emerges, as well as the discomfort of possibly losing approval. Stay with both feelings. Notice that you always have a choice.

When Your Smile Isn't Honest

We smile all the time, at work, in conversations, at strangers, during tension, even in moments of pain. But many of these smiles have little to do with joy. They're often masks, automatic habits meant to soothe others, deflect conflict, or keep us safe.

From a young age, many of us learn that smiling makes us more likable, less threatening, and more acceptable. We smile when we're uncomfortable, when we're hurt, when we disagree. Over time, the smile becomes a script: *I'm okay. You're okay. Everything's fine.*

But underneath the surface, something else may be true: *I'm anxious. I'm angry. I don't feel safe. I want to say no.*

Practice: The next time you feel yourself smiling automatically, pause. Gently tune in to your face and notice any tension in your facial muscles: your jaw, your cheeks, your eyes. What are you really feeling at that moment? What emotion is trying to surface beneath the smile?

You don't need to stop smiling altogether. But by noticing when your smile is reflexive rather than real, you begin to restore honesty to your body and presence to your communication. Sometimes, not smiling is the most honest and courageous thing you can do.

How Empathy Can Turn into Overextension

Empathy is one of the most powerful ways we connect with others. But when misunderstood, it can easily turn into something heavy, exhausting, or self-erasing.

True empathy is not about merging with someone else's pain. It's not about taking it on as your own or feeling responsible to fix, rescue, or stay entwined. Empathy is the willingness to let their experience touch you, without losing your own center.

It's a choice, not a contract. You step closer for a moment, feel what needs to be felt, offer presence, and then you step back into yourself. Many people confuse empathy with sacrifice. They believe that to truly care, they must act, solve, or stay inside the other's experience indefinitely. But this isn't empathy, it's overextension. It leads to resentment, depletion, and codependence.

Real empathy allows you to remain rooted in your own being, even as you offer understanding. It respects the separateness and sovereignty of both people. It says: *I see you, I feel with you, and I trust you to walk your own path.*

Practice: The next time you feel pulled into someone else's emotions, pause and ask yourself, Am I joining them, or merging with them?

Notice if you can stay connected to your own center while still offering presence. Real empathy honors both your heart and theirs.

Beyond Emotional Highs: What Creates Real Depth

The longing for depth is universal. We want our lives to feel meaningful, our relationships to feel substantial, our experiences to matter. But often, what we call "depth" is misunderstood.

Sometimes, in the pursuit of depth, we seek intense encounters, philosophical conversations, emotional breakthroughs, spiritual awakenings, and other big feelings. These moments feel alive.

Yet intensity is not the same as depth. Intensity can be immediate, dramatic, and consuming. But depth is quieter. It builds over time, through presence, responsibility, and the willingness to stay engaged even when nothing feels extraordinary.

When we chase depth through constant emotional highs, we may be trying to shortcut the slower, harder work of meaning-making. We may be seeking connection, trust, and aliveness, but through experiences that burn brightly and then disappear.

If you reflect on what has brought true depth to your life, it is rarely just a moment of inspiration or an intense emotional experience. It is what you have sustained: the family you've built, the friendships you have nurtured, the values you have lived by, and the work you have shaped with care. Depth is not about how intensely you feel in any given moment. It's about what lasts, what continues to shape you over time.

The Challenge of Recognizing and Expressing Needs

Identifying what you need can be surprisingly tricky. For many, the challenge begins in childhood, when you were not taught to respect your own needs or distinguish them from those of others, particularly your parents. Expressing needs as a child might have been met with shame, rejection, or the expectation to justify them. Over time, this conditioning leaves you uncomfortable with simply having needs, prompting you to hide or suppress your desires.

Natural needs, like alone time, curiosity, touch, belonging, or safety, can come to feel unnatural or even shameful. As you grow older, you may become cautious, calculating, and distrustful of the simplicity of needing or expressing what naturally arises. Over time, genuine needs for attention, affection, or relevance shift into demands, whether expressed from the perspective of being the victim or the view that "I deserve it" (identification as the aggressor). You may demand protection, recognition, closeness, loyalty, affection, trust, and the like, often driven secretly and unconsciously by fears of rejection, invisibility, or unworthiness.

Expressing your needs can feel deeply vulnerable, it means admitting you can't do it alone and trusting others to respond with care. Because of this, many people struggle to ask directly. Some turn their needs into demands, believing they are owed something and expecting others to meet those needs out of obligation. This can create tension and push others away.

Others go in the opposite direction. The shame of having unmet needs may lead to total withdrawal, convincing themselves they don't need anything at all. Or, instead of asking, they resort to taking, using control, manipulation, or emotional pressure to get their needs met without openly expressing them.

When needs stay unspoken for too long, they often intensify into what others experience as neediness: a heightened sensitivity, fear of abandonment, or constant craving for reassurance. To the receiving partner, this can feel overwhelming, like an endless set of invisible demands that are impossible to satisfy.

Healing begins by coming back to the simplicity of your needs, acknowledging them, expressing them, and making space for connection that's rooted in honesty.

Practice: Instead of rigidly listing or defining your needs, it's more valuable to explore the conditions that allow you to recognize and receive nourishment. Asking questions like, "What do I not allow myself to ask for?" or "What beliefs keep me from acknowledging my needs?" can open the door to deeper understanding. It's not just about identifying what you need to get, but also about noticing what would genuinely nourish you.

When you allow yourself to express needs openly and without drama, it becomes an act of self-love. Expressing a need signals respect for yourself and trust in others, fostering authentic connection and mutual understanding. This openness also sets up the people around you for success, making it more likely that they can meet your needs, which is essential for the other side as well.

When Strength Becomes Isolation

We often equate strength with self-reliance. We take pride in handling things ourselves, managing emotions privately, and carrying burdens quietly. But when we rely solely on our own strength, we risk disconnection, from others, from meaning, and from life itself.

Real strength isn't about being the engine of your own existence, it's about remembering that you're part of something greater. You are a vehicle, yes, but one moved by breath, by community, by purpose. Strength deepens when it flows through connection, not in spite of it.

Humility arises when you stop imagining that you have to carry everything alone. If the word humility feels too abstract, think instead of belonging, to others, to the world, to something bigger than your individual will. This awareness softens the pressure of self-reliance and opens the door to support, collaboration, and deeper meaning.

Consider a leader, a caretaker, a provider, or anyone who embodies strength. What makes that strength sustainable is not perfection or control, but connection. True connection isn't one-sided; it requires interdependence. When we share responsibility, ask for help, and allow others to matter to us, strength becomes relational, not isolating, but alive.

To Choose Is to Be Seen

Making a choice is rarely just a neutral act. Your decisions may be judged as selfish, naive, or even wrong by others, but they are reflections of where you are in a given moment. Each choice, whether it leads to clarity or confusion, success or failure, carries a message: This is where I am. This is what I'm learning. Every step you take shapes your reality and opens the door to growth.

Avoiding choice might feel safer. It can offer a temporary sense of innocence or relief, especially if you let someone else decide for you. But over time, this avoidance creates weakness. It places you in the role of a bystander in your own life, waiting to be directed instead of daring to act.

Practice: Try making choices even when they feel vulnerable. Especially then. The act of choosing reveals your needs, your preferences, your limits, and your willingness to be seen. In that exposure lies strength. When you choose, you declare: I am here. I get to participate in my life. That, in itself, is power.

Turning Feeling into Form

As your personality develops, you build an intricate web of survival strategies, ways of thinking, reacting, and speaking that help you stay safe or accepted. But in the process, you can lose the ability to see things as they are. You may sense something's off but struggle to put it into words. You may say "something feels wrong" and quickly move on, instead of slowing down and naming what's actually happening. When you don't name your experience clearly, life begins to feel vague, automatic, and out of your hands.

Naming something with precision is not about being dramatic or over-explaining. It's about reclaiming authorship. When you describe an experience with clarity, you give it shape. It stops being a fog and becomes something you can understand, work with, and move through. Naming things is an act of grounding.

One way to reclaim a sense of inner unity is by naming things for what they are. When you articulate your experiences with clarity and precision, you give them meaning and substance, allowing them to inform you. Without this practice, you may remain confused, speaking in vague headlines that lack the nuance necessary for deeper understanding.

For example, if you say, "My boundaries have been crossed," you may express a feeling, but the statement is too broad to reveal what is truly happening. Instead, statements such as "I expected to be treated with more care" or "I didn't realize the degree of responsibility I took upon myself" provide greater clarity. These specific expressions illuminate where your integrity or clarity was lost, making it easier to understand and address the situation. Naming things accurately requires practice and a commitment to precision in your words. This approach allows you to go beyond simply expressing yourself, it transforms your language into a tool for insight and growth.

Stop Waiting to Be Chosen

Waiting can feel strangely safe. You sit quietly on the edges of life, hoping to be chosen, noticed, included, without having to risk asking for what you really want.

Over time, waiting can evolve from a circumstantial choice and temporary feeling into a habitual way of being. Instead of stepping forward, you hold back. Instead of declaring "I want," you hope that someone will notice your potential, your needs, your longing, without you having to name it.

Beneath this pattern, there is often a deep fear of rejection, shame for needing in the first place, or early memories of being overlooked or punished for asking too much. Maybe you learned that being good meant being quiet. Maybe you were praised for being responsible and self-sufficient, or dismissed as naive when you dared to express desires.

So, you learned to wait. To observe. To anticipate. You became an expert at reading the room, adjusting, softening, hinting, without fully stepping into visibility.

Practice: To move out of this passive position, you must take the subtle but significant step from feeling "I can" to declaring "I want." The "can" keeps you in the background, unnoticed and undefined, while the "want" brings you into presence, placing you on the map and into belonging.

Always & Never: The Trap of Absolutes

In relationships, the words *always* and *never* appear when emotions run high. When you feel overwhelmed, helpless, or frustrated, these absolutes offer what seems like a shortcut to emphasizing the depth of what you

CHAPTER 4: THE THREADS BETWEEN US

are experiencing. Saying "You always do this" or "You never listen" feels powerful in the moment, as if the strength of the words will finally make you heard.

But absolutes have unintended consequences. They paint a totalizing picture that leaves little room for nuance or recognition of what has been good. For the person on the receiving end, it can feel defeating or unfair, erasing the moments when they did try, when they did show up.

Often, when you reach for always or never, it's because you feel too flooded to stay with the specifics. There's a fear that if you express yourself more precisely, if you admit that the hurt was in one moment, not every moment, your feelings might seem smaller, less valid, or easier to dismiss. This makes you more vulnerable because the specifics show what you needed or had difficulty with. Paradoxically, it is specificity, not exaggeration, that invites real connection.

When you move away from absolutes and speak to the immediate reality, naming the action, the feeling, and the impact, you create the conditions for dialogue. You give the other person something real to hear, rather than a blanket of judgment they must defend against.

This shift demands more vulnerability. It asks you to stay present with your feelings and your unmet needs, rather than placing them behind the armor of a sweeping indictment. It also asks you to risk being clearer, and therefore more visible.

True communication is built not on winning an argument, but on creating enough openness for change, understanding, and intimacy to occur.

Practice: The next time you feel the urge to say "always" or "never," pause. Ask yourself:

- *What exactly happened that hurt me?*
- *What need of mine feels unmet right now?*

Speaking from the present moment creates more possibility for change and more space for you to be heard.

Disappointment: A Mirror to Expectations

Take a moment to feel into the role disappointment plays in your life. Do you try to avoid disappointing others? Or do you expect others not to disappoint you? Both are signs of emotional immaturity.

Growing up means learning to tolerate disappointment, both ways. You must be willing to disappoint others and to be disappointed by them. Without this willingness, you blame others for your own unspoken or unrealistic expectations, expectations you may not even realize you are carrying.

When you expect others not to be disappointed in you, what you are often really saying is, "Please don't be angry with me. I don't want to face responsibility." But disappointment can be a profound teacher. It invites you to be honest about your needs and limitations, expressing them openly and giving others the freedom to respond, without coercion, resentment, or hidden contracts.

When disappointment becomes a persistent theme in a relationship, it points to deeper patterns. Disappointment is layered: it can be manipulative, vulnerable, insatiable, and deeply human all at once. Often, it carries an unspoken plea: "See my needs and take care of them without me having to ask."

You may find yourself overextending to avoid disappointing others, trying relentlessly to satisfy every need, until the weight becomes too heavy and resentment builds. Or you may turn disappointment inward, quietly deciding, "I am the disappointment."

Healing begins when you risk the vulnerability of naming your needs clearly, even when it feels painful or exposed. If you tend to absorb the expectations of others, healing means being willing to disappoint them, to stay true to yourself rather than living to manage their emotions.

In this space of honesty and risk, connection can return. Not a perfect connection, but something deeper, freer, and more human.

Chapter 5: Inside the Mystery of Love

Love draws us in with promises we can't fully name. We sense its power to transform us, reveal hidden parts of ourselves, and make us feel whole in ways we could never reach alone. Yet what makes love so magnetic is also what makes it elusive: it is never just one thing. It is both a deep connection and a mirror for our hopes, both a generous exchange and a web of unspoken expectations; rooted in the past and alive in the present. Love rarely speaks in one language. It can be felt in a glance, a touch, an act of care, or a silence that makes room for anothers' being. Yet the way we give and receive it is shaped by all that has come before, our history, our wounds, our longing. To notice these expressions is to open ourselves to a deeper, more nuanced way of loving. To step into this mystery is to trust that in its unfolding, we are also meeting more of who we really are.

At the heart of intimacy lives a quiet paradox: how do we love another deeply without betraying ourselves? We adapt, softening around the other's wounds, stretching to keep the bond alive. Yet if adaptation hardens into self-abandonment, resentment follows. Swing too far the other way and autonomy turns cold; we protect ourselves but lose contact. Maturity asks us to hold both: to take responsibility for our inner life while staying in contact with the person in front of us. The chapters that follow navigate this tension between connection and freedom, safety and growth, and invite us to meet it consciously rather than try to solve it.

The Many Faces of "I Love You"

"I love you." A potent and powerful sentence that carries immense emotional weight. We love to hear it and to say it, but its meaning can shift depending on the context and intention behind it.

These three simple words can express depth, vulnerability, or hidden agendas:

- I love you: I see your essence and genuinely appreciate the person you are – seeing.
- I love you: I want you to say it back to me – demanding.
- I love you: You are mine, and I am yours – demanding loyalty.
- I love you: You are special and unique – creating a dream.
- I love you: Please don't hurt me – seeking protection.
- I love you: I'm afraid to be alone – worthiness.
- I love you: You're more important than me – guilt and shame.
- I love you: You're more important than me – manipulation.

These layered meanings reveal how *I love you* can be an authentic expression of connection or a reflection of unmet needs, insecurities, or hidden motives. Becoming aware of these nuances invites you to hold love more thoughtfully, speaking from a place of greater clarity, honesty, and trust.

The Power of Acknowledging Needing Another

Needing makes us vulnerable by exposing what we feel is missing to feel safe, relevant, or more complete. At the heart of any meaningful relationship is the willingness to say, "I need you." This simple acknowledgment highlights the importance of the other for our own sense of completeness. It is crucial to feel, and perhaps say, the following to your partner: "I want to give to you, and I am ready to receive from you," or "I need you to complement me, just as I can complement something in you."

Your resistance to such statements can reveal deeper themes, such as where trust, respect, or gender-related judgments block your openness to embracing the value of the other. When spoken sincerely and without drama or romanticized notions, these words create a foundation for connection based on mutuality. They align both partners with a shared understanding of the fundamental meaning and purpose of the relationship.

The Reality of Unconditional Love

Spiritually, the belief in unconditional love is vital. It reminds us that, at our core, we are worthy of belonging without needing to earn it. Without this deeper faith, life can feel unbearably harsh and isolating.

But in human relationships, love is never truly unconditional. It comes with limits, needs, and expectations, whether spoken or unspoken. To expect unconditional love from a partner is to set both yourself and them up for disappointment. Relationships exist in the world of form: of time, desires, preferences, wounds, and histories. They require reciprocity. They ask for effort, trust, understanding, and sometimes, difficult compromises.

The sooner you can name and honor the natural conditions that exist in your relationships, the more grounded and resilient those relationships can become. Not because you have failed at love, but because you have chosen to love in the real world.

Making your conditions conscious to yourself and to your partner doesn't diminish the soul connection between you. It strengthens it. It creates space for real love to grow, not based on fantasy, but on mutual care, honesty, and trust.

Practice: Take a moment to reflect:

- What unspoken conditions do you carry into your relationships?
- What needs feel essential for you to stay open and connected?

Naming them doesn't weaken love. It makes space for love to grow.

Drama and Passion

Many relationships begin with drama and passion, which are often mistaken for depth, intensity, and aliveness. While these elements feel exciting, they are not sufficient as the cornerstone of a lasting relationship. Over time, relying on drama and passion leads to instability, as they lack the foundation of honest communication and trust needed to sustain a deep connection.

We Often Step into Roles That Make Us Resentful Later On

In relationships, feelings of betrayal often arise, even outside of major breaches like infidelity or financial misconduct. When we examine these feelings more closely, they are frequently rooted in unmet expectations. The greater the expectations you carry, the more potential there is for betrayal. Similarly, roles within relationships create a parallel dynamic. The more roles you adopt, the greater the likelihood of disappointment and resentment.

We often step into roles that are not fully aligned with who we are. These roles serve as strategies to secure love, recognition, and a sense of safety. As protective mechanisms, they lead us to unconsciously offer things we don't fully understand or even truly want to give. Beyond the foundational roles of lover and friend, it is common to take on additional roles, caretaker, teacher, replacement family, and others, that provide a sense of strength and importance within the relationship. While the intention behind these roles may be to foster love and connection, they often result in frustration and anger for both partners.

This dynamic can create a cycle where giving becomes an effort to earn love, rather than a relaxed and conscious choice. If you reflect on your own experiences, you may recognize moments when you gave not out of genuine desire but from a sense of duty or fear of losing connection. To move beyond feelings of betrayal, you must be willing to let go of these roles and the expectations tied to them.

Instead of giving out of obligation, you can begin to shift toward intentional choice. This allows for a relationship that is rooted in authenticity rather than performance, reducing the potential for resentment and the experience of betrayal. By embracing this shift, both partners can engage in a dynamic that is built on mutual respect and true emotional presence.

The Hidden Wounds Behind the Roles We Play

Roles are mainly protective strategies we develop early in life to shield ourselves from hurt and rejection. They arise from a fear of losing love and strip us of our authenticity, distancing us from our essential selves. Adopting a role, whether as the strong one, the victim, or the caretaker, comes at the cost of choice and connection. These roles perpetuate imbalance in relationships, as they prevent an honest meeting between individuals. You may pretend to be strong to hide your vulnerability or act weak to seek attention, constantly adapting to avoid rejection.

Over time, these patterns take root in your personality, spreading like a web and becoming ingrained in your sense of self. Inauthenticity, a byproduct of these roles, generates anger and pain, as deep down you recognize that expressions of superiority or inferiority are not true reflections of who you are. The wounds driving these patterns serve as reminders of what needs to be healed, while the roles you adopt are reflections of your own inner struggles, not the actions of others. Your partner or relationship may trigger the pain tied to these patterns, but the origins lie within you.

Healing begins by recognizing the roles you play, teacher, victim, entertainer, seductress, and the patterns they create, such as blaming, collapsing, or seeking recognition. By acknowledging these dynamics, you can move toward authenticity and balance in your relationships.

Trust Versus Safety: A Misunderstood Relationship

We often speak of trust and safety as if they're interchangeable, but they're not. Safety is about creating conditions where your nervous system can settle. It prevents shutdown, keeps you regulated, and makes presence possible. It's essential. But it's not the same as trust.

Trust doesn't emerge simply because you feel safe. Trust emerges when you choose to stay engaged. It's the willingness to remain in flow despite discomfort that builds real trust.

This is where many of us get stuck. You might put your trust in someone not because they've earned it, but because you're afraid to confront what you actually feel. You avoid conflict, soften your voice, or wait for their confirmation, because deep down, you don't yet trust the precision of your own intuition. You reach for safety through validation. But that reliance on external confirmation weakens your inner clarity, and trust can't grow in its absence.

In truth, trust is something we gain, lose, and gain again. It's dynamic. In a close relationship, it only takes root when you're willing to meet the other person where they are, not where you wish they were. If you cling too tightly to how you think they should act or who they should be, you trade connection for control. You may feel safer, but at the cost of something more meaningful.

And here's the tension: your partner is evolving. So are you. Through grief, healing, insight, and growth, both of you are constantly becoming. The authentic self is never static; it unravels and reshapes itself over time. The more you try to protect the relationship with rules, roles, or rigid expectations, the more you avoid deeper contact with this reality. Safety without flexibility creates walls. Trust, on the other hand, asks for movement.

What your soul longs for isn't perfect safety, it's honest, flexible trust. And that requires a shift in attitude. Romanticized ideas of how love or life should be often harden into rigid attachments. You expect a relationship, a career, or your own evolution to unfold in a certain way. But that expectation turns life into a performance, one where trust is replaced by a need to control outcomes.

The truth is that life is inherently unsafe. We build rules and systems to help us navigate it, but they can't protect us from change, loss, or the constant reshaping of what's real. Real trust only grows when you're willing to lose what you've gained, again and again. In relationships. In healing. In personal growth. Trust doesn't come from certainty, but from the quiet courage to stay open, inside the unknown.

At the same time, it's important to acknowledge that safety is often not experienced early in life. Boundaries were crossed, innocent trust was broken, and the body learned vigilance instead of ease. In such cases, safety must first be re-established somatically. By addressing heightened alertness and nervous system reactivity, the body can begin to feel safe within itself again. This inner safety is not the same as trust, but it is essential. Without it, the flow necessary for trust to emerge cannot be sustained.

Meeting Your Partner Where They Are

In long-term relationships, when partners know each other deeply, most feelings and accusations have some truth behind them. Yet instead of meeting our partner in what they notice, we often respond with defensiveness or counteraccusation.

If your partner says, "I feel you being distant or defensive," it's easy to answer with, "You're imagining things" or "You've been busy too." But what one partner perceives often holds the key to reconnection, if we can meet them where they are. That, of course, makes us vulnerable, because what they name is usually something we already sense within ourselves.

It takes courage to agree with what is being seen, to say, "Yes, maybe I have been distant" or "Something feels off between us." Acknowledging this truth brings uncertainty, but it is the only way to restore genuine closeness. Denial protects us for a moment; honesty has the potential to reconnect us.

When we allow ourselves to meet in truth rather than defense, we make space for something new to happen, for understanding, repair, and intimacy to grow where distance once stood.

Practice: The next time your partner approaches you with a feeling or realization, resist the impulse to explain or defend. Instead, pause and ask yourself: *What if what they see is true?* Try to meet them there. It will likely reveal something important for both of you.

Rewriting the Unspoken Rules of Partnership

In the early stages of a relationship, especially when you're falling in love, it's easy to form unspoken agreements without even realizing it. These silent "contracts" are shaped by your hopes, ideals, and unmet needs. They can be "I accept you the way you are," "I will always be there for you/available to you," or "all other friendships are secondary to you."

At first, they can create a sense of safety and closeness. But over time, they often lead to misunderstandings, unrealistic expectations, or quiet resentment. Because these agreements happen unconsciously, neither partner gets a chance to choose or talk through them. That can leave both people feeling let down or confused, even when no one did anything "wrong."

One of the most important steps in building a strong, lasting relationship is to bring these hidden agreements into the open. When you recognize the expectations you've been carrying, like believing your partner should always make you feel loved, safe, or needed, you can start taking responsibility for your side of the dynamic. This shift helps you move from blame to clarity.

Renegotiating your relationship means creating new, shared agreements based on who you both are now, not who you hoped each other would be at the beginning. These agreements reflect current needs and allow room to grow, adapt, and realign as life changes.

The process starts with self-reflection: What were you hoping for? What did you expect but never said out loud? What patterns are you repeating? From there, open and honest conversations with your partner can turn old assumptions into conscious choices, based on compromise, not sacrifice.

Practice: Every healthy relationship needs space to examine and update the unspoken rules that shape how you relate. No partnership thrives on perfection, it grows through shared honesty, flexibility, and the willingness to keep choosing each other as you evolve. Start by writing down a few silent expectations you've held in your relationship, things you assumed without ever saying out loud. Ask yourself: Where did this come from? Is it still relevant? Then, invite your partner into a calm, open conversation. Share your reflections and ask about theirs. Focus on listening more than fixing. The goal isn't to have perfect agreements but to create space for understanding, adjustment, and shared intention.

The Power Play of Innocence and Selflessness

At their core, all relationships are expressions of need, a dynamic where we say, "I need something from you," or, at times, "I'll give to you because fulfilling your needs meets a need within me." Yet, openly acknowledging this is difficult. Many of us associate expressing needs with punishment, whether through withheld love, humiliation, or feelings of weakness.

To avoid this vulnerability, we develop safer strategies for receiving what we need. One such strategy is to present ourselves as selfless: "Look what a good person I am. I only want to give." This dynamic often masks a deeper wish to remain innocent and avoid criticism. By pretending not to need, we shield ourselves from the perceived weakness of dependency. However, denying our needs is a denial of our humanity, creating a hidden power dynamic where the pursuit of innocence and moral superiority becomes a subtle form of control.

If you reflect on your own patterns, you may notice how this dynamic plays out in your relationships. Perhaps you give freely but secretly expect something in return, or you struggle to ask for what you need because it feels selfish or weak. True expansion happens when you allow yourself to relinquish control, embrace the uncertainty of relationships, and detach from specific outcomes.

A key step is to confront and allow feelings like anger, which, though socially condemned, often highlight inconsistencies or imbalances in relationships. If you examine your own anger, you may find that it reveals where you have been silent about your needs or where your giving has come with hidden expectations. By exploring the source of anger, you can uncover deeper truths and open the door to growth.

Letting go of the powerful role of innocence requires something more meaningful to take its place. This shift begins with recognizing the pain of self-betrayal, feeling the consequence of sacrifice and the unfulfilled realization of your potential. This pain, though disruptive, can guide you toward a deeper love for truth. While fear and setbacks are inevitable, staying in touch with the pain of self-betrayal can become a key to greater self-awareness, responsibility, and authenticity in relationships.

Care and Will: When Care Masks Disconnection from the Self

Placing too much emphasis on how much care you show toward a partner often reflects a lack of connection to your own personal will. Care can easily become a way to reward yourself with feelings of praise, recognition, importance, innocence, and righteousness. However, this behavior may signal a deeper disconnection from your true strength, will, and healthy selfishness, the qualities necessary to fulfill your own potential and sense of self-esteem.

The Difficulty and Gift of Honoring the Masculine and Feminine in Your Partner

Attraction is fueled by polarity. What draws us together is not sameness but difference, the dynamic tension between masculine and feminine. In the beginning, this polarity makes us feel both alive and safe. We are accepted by the other in a way that allows us to express our masculinity or femininity; we feel it is welcome.

(In this section, I focus on the masculine in men and the feminine in women. These terms are used interchangeably with men and women, while recognizing that both masculine and feminine exist in each of us.)

Paradoxically, what attracts us to the opposite sex can also stir feelings

CHAPTER 5: INSIDE THE MYSTERY OF LOVE

contrary to attraction, even triggering rejection. Many difficulties in relationships originate from a wounded masculine or feminine. When these essences are hurt and not easily embodied, the natural flow toward the opposite sex is interrupted. Beyond our own inner struggles, we also judge and fear the essence of the opposite sex. Generations of aggression and humiliation between men and women have left scars of distrust and disrespect.

We stop appreciating the masculine or feminine qualities of our partners, and in doing so we diminish the very polarity that once connected us. What further weakens this polarity is that, gradually, we grow more alike, meeting mostly around practical agreements and daily routines, while the deeper essence of who we are as men and women fades into the background.

Reclaiming polarity requires conscious effort. On the individual level, it may mean doing personal work to reconnect in healthy ways with our own masculine or feminine essence. On the relational level, it means honoring and supporting our partner in being seen in theirs. This is not simple. We often resist the full power that emerges when a woman stands in her feminine or a man in his masculine.

So, how can we show up for one another and support the healing process? To honor something means to know it, to understand it, and to value its complexity. On a basic level, honoring the masculine or feminine means respecting the sexuality of the other. Yet here distortion often enters. We may desire the other sexually, not from honoring, but from objectification or the pursuit of pleasure alone. In this way, the honoring becomes clouded.

Going a step beyond the sexual to the relational, it raises an essential question: How do you honor the feminine in your female partner? How do you honor the masculine in your male partner? Just as importantly, how do you diminish it? Men may criticize women in ways that dim the radiance of the feminine. Women may overlook or minimize the accomplishments of men, preventing them from shining in their masculine.

The work, then, is twofold: to reclaim your own essence and to consciously honor that of your partner. This requires humility, self-inquiry, and the courage to celebrate both your own essence and that of your partner, instead of fearing or diminishing them.

Practice: Take a moment to reflect on your relationship.

- Where do you uplift your partner's masculine or feminine essence?
- Where do you diminish it, through criticism, neglect, or indifference?
- What feelings arise in you when your partner fully embodies their masculine or feminine power? Fear? Envy? Resistance?

To open dialogue, ask each other: What would help you feel that your masculine or feminine essence is honored, recognized, or celebrated?

Sharing Expectations

Having and expressing expectations toward your partner shows that you need them and that they play an important role in your sense of fulfillment. When you resist sharing your expectations, is it due to a fear of closeness? Or does it stem from feeling undeserving to ask for what you need? By sharing your expectations, you give your partner the opportunity to meet those needs, which in turn makes them feel relevant, an essential human need. The reluctance to express expectations can often deprive relationships of clarity and mutual understanding.

But even more than that, it can create a quiet emotional distance, where your partner senses your disappointment but doesn't know why. When shared openly, expectations become a bridge, not a burden. They invite your partner into your inner world and offer a chance to co-create a relationship where both people feel seen, valued, and needed.

When Love Turns into a Scorecard

Competition often plays a subtle yet significant role in relationships, arising for various reasons. Some of these dynamics have roots in the broader battle, who's the better sex? Additionally, competition often emerges once the initial stage of falling in love has passed, and resentment and disappointment start building around unmet expectations and imperfections.

When dissatisfaction creeps in, comparison becomes a way to express discontent, particularly when you feel unable to accept differences or lack the tools to foster meaningful change. Have you ever caught yourself measuring love by comparing efforts? Relationships can slip into a transactional character, where love is tested through comparisons:

- Who loves more or less?
- Who is the better or more caring parent?
- Who contributes more around the home?
- Who is livelier and more fun?
- Who has more integrity? ... and the list goes on.

This focus on what you do versus what your partner doesn't can quietly erode goodwill, setting your partner up to fall short. In families, much of what gets done often remains invisible to the other person.

Shifting attention from what your partner isn't doing to noticing and valuing what they are doing, how they show care, where they take responsibility, and how they show up, can transform this dynamic. One of the hardest challenges in a relationship is learning to value what you contribute without diminishing your partner for what they may lack or offer in a different way.

Relationships are delicate, and comparison-driven competition is exhausting, slowly eroding trust and intimacy. Instead of measuring love or worth through this lens, shifting your focus from criticism to appreciation and from disappointment to openness can create a more constructive dynamic.

When you feel the impulse to compare, can you instead express what you need directly? Competition often masks unmet needs, and asking for what truly matters may be the key to breaking free from this cycle.

The Feeling of Being in It Together

So much of what we look for and call cooperation in relationships is really coordination. We divide tasks, share responsibilities, and manage logistics, but rarely do we touch the deeper experience of what it would mean, and feel like, to be in it together.

True togetherness is not about efficiency; it's about a shared sense of what we both care for and take care of. It's the feeling that both partners are contributing to something larger than themselves, a whole that includes both of them, and often the family they are nurturing together. When this sense of shared purpose is alive, what each gives, time, effort, attention, feels like nourishment rather than sacrifice and doesn't require the tiresome scorekeeping often found in partnerships.

Yet for many individuals who form partnerships, this experience of doing things together is missing. Even loving, well-intentioned partners find themselves competing rather than feeling we're in this together. Each waits, often silently, to be recognized and appreciated for what they bring, while quietly carrying resentment for the lack of recognition or appreciation.

When recognition is missing, the bond begins to fray. Instead of giving to the whole, to the together, we start giving for validation. Effort becomes proof, and love turns into a quiet scorekeeping of who contributes more, who cares more, who carries more.

Part of the reason togetherness feels elusive is that many of us have never truly experienced it. We are more familiar with relationships of giving and receiving, parents caring for children, or partners sacrificing for love, than with the shared experience of building and nurturing something together. This absence of "doing together" leaves many adults unsure how to co-create without collapsing into competition or dependence.

Beneath this difficulty also lies a collective and historical dimension. Generations of pain and misunderstanding between men and women have left behind layers of mistrust and quiet resentment. On both sides, there remains a lingering disrespect for what the other brings, a belief, however subtle, that my way is better or more important. When these traces of collective hurt shape the relationship, the idea of truly doing something together can feel unreal, even unsafe.

To rediscover togetherness, both partners must first acknowledge the *relevance* of what the other contributes. It's not about equality in a mechanical sense but about honoring how each part serves the whole. When you can recognize that your partner's strength, sensitivity, or steadiness complements your own, you begin to move from isolation to belonging, from rivalry to alliance.

Cooperation, then, is only the outer expression of togetherness, the practical form it takes. But without the inner sense of we are in this together, cooperation remains mechanical. True togetherness emerges when both partners orient toward the same center, giving not just to one another, but to what they are creating together.

Practice: Review the following questions. Let them settle in you, rather than looking for answers. Each question aims to evoke a feeling in you. Let the feeling come first before you answer.

- What did you see at home regarding your parents' sense of *we're in this together* versus individual contribution?
- Do you know the feeling of doing something together, not where you are giving or receiving, but setting out equally in a joint creation?
- What part of your partner's contribution do you undervalue, and where are you focused on receiving recognition?
- What would it feel like to view your shared life, your relationship, your family, as a single living whole that you both serve?
- How might this shift your sense of giving, receiving, and belonging?

Fighting: A Necessary Release

Fighting in relationships is essential. It's one of the few ways to release built-up frustration and resentment, address a sense of unfairness, diffuse overall tension, and restore balance. However, during a fight, it's difficult to connect on a deeper level. You may become consumed by emotions and focused on protecting yourself, fixated on who is right or wrong. Fights often trigger feelings of weakness, disrespect, guilt, and shame. To move beyond this, ask yourself questions like, What am I really looking for or needing? or What do I think my partner is trying to "do" to me? These questions can uncover the underlying needs and emotions, such as hurt or anger, that often fuel the fight, creating space for resolution and understanding.

Objectification: A Misunderstood Necessity

Objectification in relationships is necessary to a certain degree. It reflects the natural polarity between men and women, the needs we have of one another, and the fantasies we associate with the opposite sex. It also reveals our desire to experience certain "powers," qualities or strengths we may lack ourselves, through the other, allowing us to feel more whole. Objectification is also what makes sex sexual and exciting.

Over time, however, the fantasy element in a relationship tends to fade as partners shift from idealized figures to actual realities. Even then, objectification remains significant, as it inherently includes the roles we wish the other to fulfill to feel more at home in our own skin. These projections and exchanges of qualities between partners shape the dynamics of attraction and connection.

Sexually, objectification needs to be redefined and rediscovered throughout the course of a relationship. When partners resist engaging playfully in objectification, stagnation and boredom can set in. Respect and objectification are not mutually exclusive; rather, when embraced consciously, they can sustain intimacy and keep the connection alive.

CHAPTER 5: INSIDE THE MYSTERY OF LOVE

Sexual Desire: The Ebb and Flow of Intimacy

Our sexual desire for a partner is often put on hold or, in some cases, entirely lost. While unresolved hurt and the demands of parenting are common reasons, many other factors contribute to this decline. These may include past trauma or abuse that resurfaces later, or the over-idealization of a partner, which eventually gives way to a more realistic understanding of who they are.

Desire also reflects how connected we feel to ourselves, our own vitality, sense of aliveness, and emotional openness. It's not always about the relationship, but often about the way we feel in our own skin, how we carry stress, or how much of ourselves we've had to repress to maintain daily life. When you go numb to parts of yourself, desire becomes harder to access.

Many couples live without sexual contact for years, convincing themselves that it's unimportant or that being "just friends" is enough. While sexuality and desire naturally move through phases, it's essential not to become complacent. For most relationships, a deep, intimate connection includes sexual contact. Without it, something vital often begins to fade, intimacy becomes flatter, connection less alive.

Desire doesn't require perfection or constant passion, but it does need honesty. That includes a willingness to look at what has gone quiet in us, not just in our partner. Avoiding this conversation can quietly erode the relationship, even if everything else seems to function. Reconnecting sexually is not only about reigniting passion but also about rediscovering the part of ourselves that still longs to be touched, seen, and met.

Desire and Love

Desire and love are often mistaken for each other, yet they move in different directions. Desire reaches outward, seeking to claim, to merge, to possess. It naturally objectifies and projects, it turns the other into the vessel of our longing. Love, by contrast, allows the other to remain whole, distinct, and free.

When desire and love intertwine, they can either enrich each other or create tension. Without awareness, desire can overshadow love, bending it into a shape that serves our fantasy. But when we notice the difference, we can let love hold desire without losing respect for the other's freedom.

The Battle, Who's the Better Sex?

Men and women, both consciously and unconsciously, get caught in a battle over who has it better. This competition arises from the deep dependence and need we have for one another, without this interdependence, the battle would lack its fuel. Who's more moral? Smarter? More reliable, more mature, more oppressed, or more aggressive? The comparison extends to questions of morality, intelligence, reliability, maturity, aggression, guilt, suffering, and ultimately the question, who has life easier?

But this constant comparison makes it hard to build real trust and respect. Instead of acknowledging the unique paths, hardships, and expressions of aggression and power inherent to each sex, many view these differences as flaws to be corrected. Rather than facing the fears and vulnerabilities that feed mistrust and striving for understanding, we rush to judgment.

For example, men may feel threatened by women's anger or intuitive power, while women may fear men's physical strength or dominance. Engaging with the reality of the other would strip away the blanket judgments used for self-protection. However, if you slow down and genuinely feel the truth of the other person's experience, something changes. The judgments you've relied on to protect yourself start to fall away.

As long as you cling to the question of who suffers more or who faces more challenges, you hold on to a need to be more, more special, better, smarter, stronger, or more mature. This need to elevate yourself above the other not only perpetuates division but also blinds you to the ordinariness that unites both men and women. In overlooking this shared humanity, you miss the opportunity for true connection.

Reflecting on these themes allows you to move beyond the competition of who's better and toward a more balanced perspective on this aspect of life. You can begin to hold a more compassionate and honest view of existence, one that sees effort, sacrifice, and pain as part of the human condition, not just male or female experience. Recognizing that life is demanding for everyone can help heal divisions and foster mutual respect, rather than placing men and women in opposition.

Practice: Is there something you would add or subtract from either column in **Table 2**? As you read through these reflections, notice whether you find yourself searching for a winner in the debate of who's the better sex or if you tend to overlook certain points rather than allowing their limitations and impact to be fully felt. Both men and women face profound struggles shaped by biological, societal, and historical dynamics. When you acknowledge these realities and allow them to touch your heart, you create space for healing, respect, and connection, essential steps in overcoming the divisions that separate us.

What Men Face ...

- Men are less connected to life and therefore more inclined to look for meaning, even at the cost of their own life.
- Men are in a constant search for meaning and freedom, two opposing forces.
- Men are prone to loneliness.
- Men constantly face the loss of trust by women and the fear of women's anger and intuition.
- Men are expected to fight and defend, and risk their life if needed.
- Men are less important in the family and need to look for importance outside.
- Men have to leave their fathers and mothers, in order to step into manhood.
- Men are objectified for being strong and resilient.
- Men have to wait to be allowed to have sex.

What Women Face ...

- Women carry the main burden of commitment/sacrifice through motherhood.
- Women are objectified as being beautiful and carry the burden of having to maintain attractiveness.
- Women face the conflict of allowing independence, intelligence, and strength without losing touch with femininity and vulnerability.
- Women are prone to depression.
- Women face the continuous struggle for equal rights.
- Women face the challenge of navigating dual roles, managing societal expectations of perfection-career, family, relationships.
- Women have to leave their fathers, in order to step into womanhood.
- Women have to agree to sex.

Table 2. The difficulties both sexes face at various stages of life

The Weight of Words Between Women and Men

In moments of connection, especially during conflict, speech carries weight. Often, women tend to express what feels true in the moment. What they say reflects their current emotional landscape, and as that landscape shifts, so can the truth they convey. This doesn't make their words inconsistent, it reflects a natural emotional responsiveness and openness to change.

Men, by contrast, often struggle more in these moments. Their words are filtered through an internal sense of obligation and anticipated consequence. When speaking to a partner, they may hesitate, carefully weighing how their words might be received or what they might commit to. This caution can sometimes make their communication seem guarded or even less trustworthy, not because they intend to deceive, but because speaking a truth, for them, feels like taking on a contract. They want to be sure they can stand by what they say.

These differing rhythms of communication can create tension: one partner needing to express and evolve in real time, while the other moves slowly, speaking only when they feel certain. Understanding these differences can ease miscommunication and make space for more compassion during emotionally charged moments.

Taking Feedback

Giving to your partner or doing things for them is one of the core exchanges in any relationship. But giving isn't always simple. It often comes with mixed feelings. You may prefer to give on your own terms, deciding what, when, and how, rather than responding directly to what your partner needs or asks for. This can make it hard to hear feedback about your giving, especially if it feels like your effort isn't appreciated.

When giving is driven by hidden motives like seeking validation, avoiding guilt, staying emotionally distant, or doing what you think you're "supposed" to do, it becomes harder to receive feedback openly. Even gentle feedback can feel like criticism or rejection. In these moments, it takes effort to remain curious and caring instead of slipping into resistance or withdrawal.

On the other hand, when your giving comes from genuine care and choice, not fear or obligation, you're more likely to be open to hearing how your actions were received. Feedback becomes less of a threat and more of a bridge, an opportunity to understand your partner more deeply and strengthen the connection between you.

Practice: When you catch yourself resisting feedback, pause and ask:

- What am I really seeking through my giving?
- Am I trying to avoid feeling vulnerable or uncertain?
- Is this a quiet test of whether I'm loved or trusted?
- Are unconscious gender roles shaping how I respond?

Reflecting on these questions can help reveal the deeper patterns at play, and open the door to a more honest, caring, and mutual relationship dynamic.

Codependency: Beyond the Negative Stigma

Codependency is often criticized in public discourse, where we're told we should strive to be independent individuals. However, accepting codependency as a natural part of how we relate, shaped by our personality, needs, and survival strategies, can help us grow in humility and better understand who we've become.

Rather than adopting rigid ideas about what relationships should look like, which often tell us little about ourselves or what we're truly capable of, embracing codependent tendencies can actually support personal growth. Have you considered how your own patterns of dependence shape your relationships? This acceptance serves the greater purpose of knowing yourself. After all, you can only examine what you accept. Whatever you reject remains hidden and unfamiliar.

Commitment and the Fear of Losing Ourselves

Many of us long for deep connection, to a person, a purpose, a path. But commitment, which makes this possible, can feel loaded. It's often tangled with fear of losing freedom, of failing someone, or of being trapped in something we didn't fully choose.

From a young age, we learn to associate commitment with obligation. Once you commit, you're expected to follow through, no matter how you feel. This turns commitment into a test of loyalty, where breaking the agreement feels like betrayal. Guilt and shame often follow.

In response, you might overcommit to prove you belong, or avoid commitment altogether to protect your independence. In both cases, fear drives the decision, not genuine choice. But commitment, at its best, is not about control. It's about depth.

When chosen consciously, commitment reflects maturity. It says: I am willing to show up fully, to share power, to speak my truth, and to listen to yours. It respects both connection and individuality. In this light, commitment becomes a living practice, not a fixed contract, but an ongoing dialogue between who you are and what you value.

What if commitment wasn't about locking something in, but about staying present to what matters most, even as it evolves? This shift transforms commitment from a source of pressure or fear into a space for truth, growth, and intimacy.

Trust and Betrayal: Moving Beyond Fixed Roles

When trust is broken through betrayal, rebuilding it requires curiosity and a willingness to embrace movement. Instead of clinging to old expectations or ideals, you must ask, *What didn't I want to see or know?* and remain open to understanding who the other person is or is becoming now. Betrayal often shatters the static picture you held of the relationship, forcing you to confront uncomfortable truths about yourself and your partner.

Many couples get stuck in a dynamic where the one who betrayed is expected to prove their worth, pay through guilt, and seek forgiveness, while the other assumes the role of the innocent with moral superiority. This imbalance keeps both partners trapped in rigid roles, seeking refuge in blame or static images of the past, which blocks vulnerability and genuine reconnection.

Regaining trust requires moving beyond these roles and exploring the deeper causes of the betrayal, as well as the evolving nature of the relationship. Trust grows when you face the discomfort of change, allow space for new insights, and remain curious about the possibilities of reconnection.

Flirting: The Unspoken Message

Flirtation is an exciting way to connect with the opposite sex and gain attention. When you flirt without the intention of pursuing a meaningful relationship, however, you fail to take the other person seriously. Flirtation, in this context, sends the message: "I can play with you, but I don't truly take you seriously."

This collective behavior places undue importance on our own sex while subtly demeaning the other. It creates a dynamic where the interaction becomes superficial, prioritizing self-gratification over viewing the other as an equal.

Making Our Partners Happy: A Power Lost

At the beginning of a relationship, we often feel a kind of emotional superpower: the sense that we can make our partner happy. This mutual sense of purpose and possibility builds closeness and fuels the connection.

But as life gets harder, this "superpower" starts to fade. When our love or effort goes unnoticed or is even rejected, we begin to question our impact on the other. Doubt creeps in. We might pull away, protect ourselves, or look for validation elsewhere.

Giving becomes vulnerable when it isn't seen or appreciated, it brings up old fears of rejection or not being enough. But instead of shutting down, both partners have a role to play in keeping the connection alive. That means noticing each other's efforts, staying open, and letting love flow both ways. This exchange, of presence, care, and recognition, makes a relationship strong and lasting.

The Collective Side of Struggles

We often think our relationship challenges are personal. But many of them are shaped by larger forces, like society, culture, and family history. These collective influences shape how we feel, act, and relate to others, often without us realizing it.

Some of the hardest emotions, like guilt, rage, distrust, or helplessness, don't start with us. They're carried through generations, passed down in families, shaped by gender roles, or rooted in cultural trauma. For example, if one partner carries the imprint of sexual trauma passed through generations of women, healing becomes a shared question. Is choosing a safe partner enough? Or does healing also require facing this pain together, recognizing that it's part of a much larger story?

Working with collective pain in a relationship takes honesty and humility. It asks us to face emotions that may not be "ours" in a personal sense, but still live in us. This isn't about taking the blame for what others have done. It's about showing up with care and a willingness to be part of the healing. When we avoid this kind of reflection, we often repeat the same painful cycles.

These inherited burdens can weigh down the hopeful energy that comes with new love. Falling in love is a beautiful start, but it's not enough to sustain a relationship over time. What helps us grow together are qualities like trust, friendship, and respect. These build the foundation we need to face both our personal wounds and the larger stories we carry.

Real connection means being willing to explore not only who we are but also what shaped us. Healing happens when we face that truth, together.

The Fear of Losing Yourself in Love

The fear of losing yourself is present in all close relationships. Love often asks for compromise, adjustment, and mutual care, but these necessary acts can, at times, create distance from your own inner voice. Maintaining connection to yourself becomes an ongoing practice.

Sometimes, that reconnection happens outside the relationship: through therapy, solo experiences, creative pursuits, or time with friends who remind you of who you are at your core. But just as often, it happens within the relationship itself. Being in connection challenges you to refine your voice, clarify your boundaries, and rediscover what feels true.

It's easy to place the blame for losing yourself on your partner, but in truth, no one can guard your sense of self for you. The invitation is not to be on the defensive, but to stay in relationship with both yourself and the other.

Wounds as Pathways to Growth

Most of us carry wounds that shape how we navigate life and relationships. Perhaps the goal is not to end the struggle but to care for our wounds in a conscious and responsible way. Every relationship, at its core, is also a meeting of wounds. For instance, someone grappling with guilt may find themselves partnered with someone who struggles with distrust, setting the partnership up for hurt and misunderstanding.

Becoming aware of the wounds you bring into your relationships allows you to take responsibility for them, rather than projecting them onto your partner. Acknowledging that all relationships involve this meeting of wounds might reduce overly romanticized notions of love, but it also reframes relationships as spaces for growth and mutual healing. Letting go of rigid truths or the need to be right allows you to approach your wounds, and those of your partner, with compassion. When you do so, you create a foundation for deeper connection, where a love relationship becomes a place of healing rather than a romanticized refuge from pain.

Necessary Lies

Lying often begins as a way to maintain a sense of control over vulnerability and uncertainty. Early in life, many of us learn that honesty can come at a cost, exposing us to judgment, rejection, or loss. In response, lying becomes a subtle form of protection, a way to shield parts of ourselves that feel too fragile or unworthy to be seen.

At first glance, lying seems to create safety. It smooths over conflicts, avoids uncomfortable truths, and offers a temporary sense of power over unpredictable situations. Yet beneath the surface, every lie, no matter how small, echoes a deeper message: *I am not safe being myself.* Over time, this internalized belief can erode self-esteem and cultivate a quiet distrust of life itself, reinforcing the fear that authenticity will not be met with acceptance.

Freedom, however, is intimately tied to honesty. When truth is hidden or distorted, freedom remains out of reach because part of the self must always be managed, disguised, or suppressed. True freedom, feeling at ease in your own skin and in the presence of others, requires the courage to risk honesty, not as a moral achievement but as an act of self-liberation.

The movement toward healing is not about forcing radical transparency or discarding all forms of self-protection overnight. It begins with noticing where old patterns of hiding still operate and where they no longer serve your deeper longing to be real.

Small, genuine moments of honesty, especially when they feel vulnerable, gradually rebuild trust in life and in yourself. They make it possible to experience a different kind of safety: one that does not rely on hiding but on the quiet strength of being seen and remaining whole.

Your Partner Should Love and Accept Your Family

It's natural to have contentious relationships with your family of origin, parents and siblings. These long-term relationships go through ups and downs, marked by stretches of closeness and distance. At times, you may feel angry or resentful toward family members, and out of love and loyalty, your partner might join you in this resentment.

The more your partner can love and accept your family of origin, even when you feel angry, distant, or resentful, the stronger the foundation of your relationship becomes. While it may initially feel supportive when your partner aligns with your struggle, it can actually become an emotional burden.

You are allowed to have conflicts with your family and move through different stages of closeness over the course of your life. But it's unnecessary, and often unhelpful, for your partner to be pulled into this dynamic. Instead, their ability to maintain neutrality and compassion toward your family can foster a sense of balance and stability in your relationship. It creates space for you to process your own experience without feeling the need to protect, defend, or justify, and ultimately strengthens the trust and emotional safety between you.

Love, Projection, and the Reality That Follows

Most of the time, we blindly fall in love, and that's probably an evolutionary necessity. If we fully understood the other person right away, it might make it harder to form such a strong connection. In those early days, we often believe the relationship will completely fulfill us on every level, without seeing the limitations or compromises that come with it.

But as time goes on and your partner's personality reveals itself in its complexity, you begin to face their needs and demands. These require compromise and sometimes even sacrifice, which can feel like a loss of freedom. Have you ever noticed an inner struggle between your desire for independence and the realities of being in a relationship? This push and pull is a natural part of long-term connection, requiring reflection on what is being projected onto your partner versus what is truly unfolding between you.

Often, we project not just hopes but unmet parts of ourselves, desires we haven't claimed, security we long for, or ideals we were taught to chase. Over time, seeing your partner more clearly can feel disappointing, but it's also the beginning of true intimacy. That's when love shifts from fantasy to something rooted in reality. The invitation is to trade illusion for understanding and to relate not to who you imagined, but to the real person standing in front of you.

Meeting Someone Who Can Carry Their Own Cross

We meet someone most fully when they can bear the weight of their own life. This doesn't mean being free of pain or difficulty, but having the capacity to manage it without making another responsible for it.

A partner who can hold their own cross stands beside you as an equal, not as someone to be rescued or who rescues you. They can share their vulnerability without collapsing into it, and they can witness yours without trying to take it away. Such meeting points create space for love to deepen because they are rooted in mutual respect and personal responsibility.

The Highest Potential

Many relationships begin with the romantic hope that one partner will help the other reach their "highest potential." It's an alluring idea, that you will lovingly guide your partner toward the person they were meant to become.

When you choose a partner for their potential, you are not truly choosing who they are, you're choosing a future version of them that may never exist. Over time, this creates quiet resentment. You may hold it against them for not becoming who you imagined, forgetting that your vision was never theirs to fulfill.

At its core, this is a subtle power play. The one who "recognizes" the other's potential places themselves above them, waiting for growth that only they have defined. In doing so, both partners lose the chance to meet each other as equals, in the reality of who they are today.

The Ideal of Being Best Friends in Love

In intimate relationships, the ideal of being best friends, with no secrets and complete honesty, is often seen as a goal. But practicing total exposure of our inner world, its light and shadow, requires time, space, and emotional capacity for understanding and processing.

Committed relationships rely not only on emotional intimacy but also on functioning as a couple, a family, and a social unit in the larger world. The full expression of every feeling, doubt, or desire cannot always be held within the relationship, just as we struggle at times to hold the full complexity of our own inner lives.

Still, the aspiration remains: to cultivate as much openness and vulnerability as possible while respecting the natural boundaries of what can be shared, received, and integrated in any given moment. True intimacy doesn't demand total exposure, it asks for presence, compassion, and the ongoing willingness to reveal ourselves honestly, piece by piece.

The Many Faces of Separation

Separation is a central theme in our inner and relational lives. It often hides in plain sight, woven into our personality, our defenses, and the subtle ways we try to manage closeness and distance. The structure of our personality, while meant to protect us and get our needs met, often becomes the very thing that creates disconnection. Its strategies, such as manipulation, withdrawal, and control, may serve us in the short term, but they also keep us separate.

In the personal and often unconscious ways we each create separation, sometimes we push others away because we feel hurt. Sometimes it's righteousness or moral superiority that gives us the sense we're entitled to stay closed. Other times, it's the refusal to resolve conflict, even when resolution is possible. The dynamic is familiar: we find ourselves oscillating between feeling superior or inferior, and either way, the result is disconnection.

What makes this so difficult to untangle is that the separation often feels justified. We tell ourselves we're right. We protect our pride. But underneath, there's still a subtle loneliness, a sense of something unfinished. The wound remains unhealed, and the separation persists.

At the heart of this inquiry are a few essential questions:

- How do I create separation with people?
- Do I usually push people away, or do I just not allow them to come close again?
- How do I justify moving away?
- What is needed from me to allow for completion to take place, even if it doesn't mean reconciliation or closeness?

When we allow ourselves to be seen, to expose the parts we usually hide, we stop holding on. Something softens. And in that softening, the inner separation begins to dissolve. That shift is not just internal; it also affects our ability to reconnect with others.

Reflect on specific examples of unresolved tension, moments where something was left incomplete between ourselves and another. Where we didn't reach out. Where we didn't allow the other to reach us. Ask yourself: What would be needed to reconnect, not necessarily to "make up," but to come to a sense of internal completion?

These reflections matter because we all create separation in some form, especially when we feel hurt, misunderstood, or powerless. It can also show up in subtler ways, like when we tell ourselves we don't need help, insisting on doing things alone. That too is a way of keeping others out.

Separation isn't always loud. It's often quiet, folded into pride, fear, shame, or the longing not to depend. But once we start to see it clearly, we can begin to take responsibility for it. And from there, something new becomes possible.

Separation as a Path to Understanding

The theme of separation exists in almost all relationships, sometimes quietly in the background and sometimes as an urgent issue. While it doesn't always lead to an actual breakup, it remains a difficult topic to discuss, as acknowledging it makes the unspoken tension visible to all. A useful question to ask yourself is: What part of myself would I wish to reclaim if I were to separate? Every relationship requires compromises and adaptations, which inevitably shape and sometimes limit our individuality. When these compromises become too painful, or when we feel we have drifted too far from who we once were, or who we aspire to be, separation can seem like the only way to regain that lost sense of self.

When separation happens, it often comes with pain, blame, or urgency, keeping us stuck, or pushing us to jump into a new relationship without fully understanding what went wrong. Yet separation, whether real or contemplated, can become a powerful invitation to grow.

For example, one partner might look back and realize they never truly voiced their needs, hoping instead their partner would intuit them. The other might see how they avoided conflict to keep the peace, but in doing so, created emotional distance. These reflections don't erase the pain but can transform the ending into a space of learning.

Partners are best served by acknowledging that the relationship's failure is a shared responsibility. This includes recognizing how your love changed, how your needs evolved, and how aspects of your personality may have negatively influenced the relationship. Accountability is often made harder by the practical and emotional weight of separation, dividing assets, managing finances, and, when children are involved, facing the pressure, and at times shame, of parenting alone. These realities add to the strain and often obscure the potential for learning.

Practice: The following questions can help you understand yourself more deeply. Consider the stage of life you were in when you met your partner. What emotional or practical circumstances shaped your connection? Were there things you noticed but chose to overlook? The ideals of love and relating that you brought into the relationship may have had a profound influence, were they realistic, or did they carry unspoken expectations?

Over time, patterns worth exploring tend to emerge. Were you waiting for your partner to change? Were there aspects you disrespected or avoided confronting? Did you hold back parts of yourself, love, time, closeness, even commitment? Were there places where the balance in the relationship shifted, leaving one partner feeling superior or inferior?

Consider, too, what your partner may have been offering that you weren't ready to receive, and vice versa. Did you conceal fears, expectations, or doubts? When were you not true to yourself, pretending, or clinging to roles or hopes that no longer served the relationship?

By exploring these questions with honesty and compassion, you may uncover patterns that extend beyond this specific relationship. Separation, then, becomes not just an end but an important pathway, toward future relationships, but also the old one, and toward personal growth, and toward reclaiming what may have been lost in the process of adapting to love.

Divorce: When Projections Break but Nothing Rebuilds

Over time, projections we hold for our partners begin to fall away, and the relationship either deepens into something more real or begins to rupture. Divorce is one outcome of that rupture.

It's not always about falling out of love. More often, it's the collapse of the fantasy that once held everything together. In the beginning, we may not yet know ourselves well enough to choose a partner clearly. We choose through the filter of what we long to heal, become, or be rescued from. And our partner often does the same. For a while, those projections can sustain the relationship, but only temporarily.

As daily life unfolds, filled with responsibilities, parenting, financial strain, or simply the passage of time, we begin to see the other person more clearly. Not the imagined self-savior or perfect match, but the full, complex human being in front of us. When there hasn't been room to grieve what's been lost or to renegotiate what's real, the result isn't just disillusionment, it's emotional starvation.

In some relationships, projection gives way to intimacy, and the work begins to meet one another anew. But in others, what emerges is a quiet sense that something essential is missing, not in the partner, but within oneself. And when this feeling goes unnamed or unexplored, divorce may feel like the only available act of self-reclamation.

What we often seek in leaving is not just escape, but coherence: a way to return to a felt sense of wholeness that somehow got buried beneath the weight of unmet expectations and unspoken grief. Divorce, then, is not just an end. It can be a search for truth, clarity, and a different kind of belonging.

Appendix A - Therapy: A Space for Reconnection

Therapy, at its essence, is a space for reconnection, with yourself, within relationships, and with the layers of humanity that often remain hidden. It is not about achieving perfection or chasing an idealized version of life but about sitting with what is, untangling layers of conditioning and pain, and embracing the complexity of being human.

Therapy invites vulnerability as a path to wholeness and encourages the exploration of authenticity as a dynamic, unfolding process. It fosters clarity, courage, and integrity, helping you live, love, and relate in ways that feel aligned.

It is an expression of love; without it, nothing truly meaningful can happen in the room. The absence of love is at the root of the distortions we struggle with in life. When a therapist lacks the capacity to love the client, the process cannot go deep, it remains technical, offering structure but failing to reach what truly needs healing.

When Therapy Feels Therapeutic

Therapy works best when you approach it with curiosity about your inner world, feeling it to be meaningful and relevant. When therapy feels therapeutic to you, healing takes place. This only happens, however, when you begin to see your essence and purpose more clearly. Without this context, you risk becoming lost in cycles of repression and avoidance, trying to focus on how to fit in. Too often, therapy focuses solely on wounds rather than addressing the deeper essence of who you are.

Different therapeutic settings offer varying degrees of potency and potential for transformation. With this in mind, it's helpful to distinguish between individual, couples, and group work. Of course, other reflective, guiding, and healing spaces exist, such as family therapy or parental guidance, which are not covered here.

Individual Therapy: Reclaiming the Self

Individual therapy provides a safe space to reconnect with parts of yourself that have been silenced by trauma, fear, or the pressures to conform. Through this work, you can rediscover your inner voice and begin to differentiate between what is authentically yours and what has been shaped by external influences.

This process involves exploring unresolved trauma, conditioned beliefs, and the fears that drive behaviors and decisions. It encourages you to reconnect with your emotions, intuition, and the wisdom of your body. By fostering vulnerability, clarity, and authentic expression, individual therapy helps you create a life that feels meaningful and true to who you are.

Couples Therapy: The Gift of Relating

Couples therapy offers a profound exploration of the challenges and opportunities inherent in intimate relationships. Relationships are spaces for healing, growth, and self-understanding through the presence of another. They invite vulnerability, mutual respect, and the continuous understanding and negotiation of needs, values, and differences.

This therapeutic work goes beyond resolving conflicts; it fosters deeper trust and connection. Couples explore the patterns, roles, and fears that shape their dynamics, as well as the ways they give and receive love. The process encourages honest communication, deep listening, and the courage to move beyond individual needs toward shared growth.

Through this work, couples learn to embrace the imperfections of both themselves and their partners. They begin to view relationships not as transactional but as spaces for mutual discovery, allowing for greater intimacy and connection.

Group Therapy: Healing Through Collective Experience

Group therapy creates a powerful space for healing and growth within the collective energy of a group, a dynamic unavailable in individual settings. It provides a unique opportunity to witness yourself through the experiences of others, offering new perspectives and insights.

These settings encourage participants to safely reconnect with their hearts, express their truths, and explore their shadows. The shared intention and collective presence amplify the healing process, fostering a profound sense of belonging and transformation.

By participating in group therapy, you are reminded that you are not alone in your struggles. You witness the courage of others, which inspires your own, creating a space for healing that is greater than the sum of its parts.

Therapy as an Invitation to Sit with What Is

Therapy is not about fixing what is broken but about learning to sit with what hurts and allowing it to teach you. It encourages you to let go of the urge to run from pain or seek quick solutions, instead inviting you to meet your discomfort with curiosity and respect. The pain itself often holds the key to healing, as it is often related to longing.

Whether through individual sessions, couples work, or group retreats, therapy offers a profound invitation to explore life's complexities, embrace shadows, and deepen connection. It serves as a pathway to rediscover humanity, live with integrity, and cultivate a life enriched by authenticity and meaning.

Appendix B - Further Reading

This book is inspired by my professional work with clients and groups, my personal life experiences, and many outstanding thinkers, whom I want to mention below. These works offer depth, perspective, and pathways into the themes explored throughout this book.

Deida, David
  Dear Lover: A Woman's Guide to Men, Sex, and Love's Deepest Bliss
  A poetic and spiritually oriented guide for women seeking deeper intimacy, presence, and embodied love.
  The Way of the Superior Man
  A modern classic on masculine purpose, polarity, and spiritual growth within relationships, offering insight into intimacy and responsibility.

Frankl, Viktor E.
  Man's Search for Meaning
  A profound reflection drawn from Frankl's experience in concentration camps, exploring suffering, resilience, and the human search for purpose through logotherapy.

Hellinger, Bert
  Peace Begins in the Soul
  An accessible introduction to Hellinger's systemic approach to family dynamics and belonging.

Hillman, James
The Myth of Analysis
A critique of traditional psychotherapy and an argument for returning psyche to imagination and myth.
The Soul's Code
Hillman proposes that each life is shaped by an innate "calling" or daimon, offering a mythopoetic view of identity and purpose.

Hollis, James
Creating a Life: Finding Your Individual Path
A call to personal responsibility and individuation, addressing midlife transitions and psychological maturity.
The Broken Mirror: Refracted Visions of Ourselves
An examination of the many selves we contain and the psychological patterns that fragment identity.

Judith, Anodea
Eastern Body, Western Mind
A comprehensive integration of Western psychology and the chakra system, exploring how developmental stages map onto the body.

Keen, Sam
Fire in the Belly: On Being a Man
A powerful inquiry into masculine psychology, desire, purpose, and the emotional injuries of men seeking authentic expression.

Levine, Peter A. (with Ann Frederick)
Waking the Tiger: Healing Trauma
A foundational work on somatic trauma healing that introduces body-based recovery and nervous-system regulation.

Liebermeister, Svagito R.
The Roots of Love: A Guide to Family Constellation

A clear and practical overview of family constellation work, illustrating how systemic entanglements shape relationships and identity.

Lipton, Bruce H.
The Biology of Belief
A groundbreaking exploration of epigenetics and the power of belief, showing how thoughts and emotions influence the body on a cellular level.

Osho
The Book of Understanding
Reflections on awareness, conditioning, and freedom, inviting readers toward clarity, presence, and inner truth.

Peterson, Jordan B.
Maps of Meaning: The Architecture of Belief
A dense but insightful integration of psychology, mythology, and philosophy exploring how humans create meaning and confront chaos.

Spezzano, Chuck
If It Hurts, It Isn't Love
Offers psychological and spiritual principles for transforming patterns of fear and dependency in intimate relationships.

Stein, Murray
Jung's Map of the Soul
A clear, structured introduction to Jungian psychology, covering archetypes, the Self, ego, shadow, and individuation.

APPENDIX B - FURTHER READING

For additional writings and information about individual, couples, and group work, you are welcome to visit
arielkarmeli.com

www.ingramcontent.com/pod-product-compliance
Lightning Source LLC
Chambersburg PA
CBHW020939090426
42736CB00010B/1197